PHOTO LIBRARIES
& AGENCIES

PHOTO LIBRARIES & AGENCIES

DAVID ASKHAM

 **BFP BOOKS** London

A catalogue record for this book is available from the British Library

ISBN 0-907297-49-8

Published by BFP Books, Focus House,497 Green Lanes, London N13 4BP.
Printed and bound in Great Britain by Polestar Wheatons Ltd

AUTHOR'S DEDICATION

This book is dedicated to serious photographers everywhere who aspire to see their work published, either by their own direct efforts, or through the medium of third party photo libraries or agencies. It is also dedicated to their spouses or partners who, like my own dear wife Shirley, share in so much of the work, but who rarely earn a byline or credit. A great deal of cooperation and team effort is deployed before they can enjoy the unalloyed pleasure of seeing their pictures in print.

CONTENTS

Introduction: The Journey Ahead

Welcome to this new book on photo libraries and agencies! So much has happened since I researched my first book on this subject, over ten years ago, that it is difficult to know where to begin.

So, I am first going to make several important assumptions. I will assume that you are one of three types of photographer:

- Fresh from college with loads of theory and great ambitions;
- An experienced professional photographer;
- A competent part-time freelance photographer.

I am also going to assume that you are keen to make money from your best pictures. Otherwise, why else would you have bought this book?

Realistic expectations

There is one further assumption – that some of you have become disappointed by your relative lack of success (in terms of picture sales) as a freelance photographer when dealing directly with clients and markets.

Take comfort: you are not alone. Many thousands of photographers tread this path every year, though sadly most give up, disillusioned. But you are one of the enterprising minority who have discovered the existence of photo libraries and agencies – the subject of this book. So you may be thinking: "If only I could find a quick route into this magical world, my problems would disappear."

But why should a commercial library succeed in selling your pictures when you have already failed? The answer is quite simple. They have expert knowledge of what the market demands and have a business organisation geared to capitalise on that knowledge. They also maintain extremely high standards because, without them, even they would have difficulty in generating and sustaining business.

"So, if photo libraries are so successful," I hear you cry, "how can I tap into their success? Or better still, how can I adopt their methods and run a successful library of my own?"

Unfortunately there are no quick answers to those pertinent questions, and that is one reason why this book has been written. I strongly believe that success as a freelance photographer can be significantly enhanced once the reader acquires a sound appreciation of how good picture libraries operate.

Success also requires an intelligent understanding of the ever-changing marketplace for photographs. But that is only part of the story. Don't forget that finely honed skills as a photographer are essential. Without the highest professional standards, you really are wasting potential clients' – and your own – time and money trying to penetrate the competitive world of commercial photography.

Photographic standards

Although we will return to the subject of standards later in the book, it is worth a brief diversion right now.

Many libraries complain of receiving poorly exposed and unsharp colour transparencies from hopeful contributors. "Why do photographers not edit their work properly before submitting it?" they frequently complain.

With the high quality cameras and lenses available today, there really is no excuse for producing shoddy work and expecting it to be accepted, no matter what the subject or circumstances.

Other photographers fail to understand the specialised nature of some photo libraries and send quite unsuitable subjects.

Such basic mistakes – poor technical quality and the submission of irrelevant photographs – just stamps a novice contributor as unprofessional. It also tarnishes the image of all freelances.

Of course, the situation is not all gloom. Many readers will already be experienced professional or semi-pro photographers in their own right, maybe having worked for some time in one of many specialised fields. The technical standards of their work will probably be beyond reproach. Yet when they come to consider marketing their photographs – possibly obtained as a by-product from other assignments – through a library, they too may well encounter disheartening difficulties.

Pictures produced for one purpose do not necessarily meet the requirements of art directors or editors who have their own constraints and preferences. For example, tightly composed photographs which are ideal for some commercial applications may be totally unsuitable for use in projects where other graphic elements have to be combined.

These observations merely illustrate the need for knowledge of the wider or specialist applications served by the appropriate photo libraries.

The range of photo libraries

The question then arises: what are appropriate photo libraries?

Libraries cover an almost unimaginable range of subjects. Some are major general libraries with many different subject sections. Others tend to specialise in the subjects they cover, possibly dealing with only one country or geographic region, or with a niche subject area like aerial photography or horticulture.

Matching your photographs to an appropriate library can be a daunting but necessary task. It is a crucial decision which should not be rushed. Many a photographer has hastily signed up with a library on the basis of noting its by-line against illustrations in magazines or newspapers, only to rue the decision later.

Choosing an appropriate photo library is such an important subject that an entire chapter is devoted to it. However, it is worth observing here that the bigger photo libraries have become increasingly selective in who they take on as new contributing photographers. The reason is simple. So many aspects of their stock have been covered, and are continually being refreshed, by trusted photographers already on their books. It is understandable that they are reluctant to sign on new photographers unless they show quite exceptional merit or can fill possible niche areas in the library.

Those overstocked libraries also try to weed out the potential time-wasters by demanding to see several hundred pictures at the outset.

The aim of this book

So what is this book all about? Essentially the aim is to demystify the picture library business by providing accurate and useful information which will enable keen and competent photographers either to set up their own successful photo libraries or, alternatively, to become productive contributors to one or more established commercial libraries.

It is intended that the book should be a complete guide so that, at the end, a photographer can enter the photo library world with confidence, understanding and real expectations of success. This aim is quite ambitious because, as individuals, we are all different and see the world in different ways. So, while the book contains most of the information needed – certainly as a first step – it would be misleading to presume that additional sources of help would not be beneficial.

Further assistance and information can be found, for example, in the monthly *Market Newsletter* published by the BFP (Bureau of Freelance Photographers) which contains timely information on selected and newsworthy photo libraries. Likewise BAPLA (British Association of Picture Libraries and Agencies) provides a useful information pack, for a modest fee, to aspiring contributing photographers. There are other sources that will be mentioned later in the book.

A decade of change

Although photo libraries have been in existence for many years – at least one since the beginning of the 20th century – most have been launched during the past 25 years and new ones continue to enter the market all the time. Some are very young indeed and have barely had time to establish themselves. But those which have been in business for ten years or more will have witnessed quite remarkable changes. Let us look at some of the more significant of these.

Possibly the most influential change has been the introduction of affordable computerisation into photo libraries. As a result of equipping offices with networked personal computers, library administration and picture delivery has been transformed. The whole process is now more efficient, stock control systems are up-to-date, accurate and complete, and accounting is greatly simplified.

It is difficult to visualise the significance of these improvements unless you could flash back to the time when typewriters, or even manual methods, were used for the preparation of all documentation. Administering fees received was a tedious task and photographers' payments were often subject to delay. There is less excuse for delays today, provided managers are disciplined and efficient.

Telecommunications now play an increasingly important role. Fax machines have largely displaced telex systems, while e-mail is serving as an economical means of communicating with global markets.

But it is not only data transmission which has revolutionised picture library transactions; the digitisation of photographic images now enables remote clients to view pictures swiftly without the original photographs

Use of architectural elements provides an original view
of Sydney, Australia across Darling Harbour.   **David Askham**

ever leaving the library. With continuing improvements in technology, there will soon be no reason why end-users will ever need access to original colour transparencies at all, provided adequate commercial and copyright safeguards can be exercised.

The ease with which images can be digitally manipulated is a development not without problems. Everyone is familiar with the digital removal of unwanted objects, even people, to suit a newspaper picture editor's whims. Where the publisher owns the copyright to the image, there is less of a problem (except for moral and historical issues). But difficulties arise if a client attempts to alter an image supplied on loan from a photo library. In many cases minor adjustments may not cause any trouble. However, it is essential that prior approval for such manipulative action is sought.

Royalty-free images

Another major change has been the impact of relatively cheap collections of royalty-free stock images distributed on CD-ROM. The specialist companies that distribute these usually buy the copyright of photographs for a fairly low fee, or may reimburse photographers with royalties based on actual sales. They then compile themed CDs and sell them direct to graphic designers or other such users. Corbis, which is profiled in Chapter 4, has a growing division specialising in selling royalty-free images.

Some people contend that direct sales of pictures to editors or designers must erode the traditional business of photo libraries. Possibly so, but not in markets where exclusivity is sought by clients.

Publishing has become much easier as a result of the arrival of fast modern personal computers with user-friendly graphical interfaces. Specialist publishing software is widely available at relatively low cost and has encouraged the launch of a whole new generation of low circulation publications. New magazines, low print-run books and other commercial literature has appeared on the market when previously its economic viability would have been questionable.

The growth of such publications has undoubtedly contributed to the growth of demand for library images. This is a small but healthy development, particularly if the demand continues to be for new imagery.

The growth of competition

A group magazine editor once described to me how his shelves were laden with photo library catalogues and how he was embarrassingly spoiled for choice. Ten years ago, only a small minority of the biggest and most prosperous photo libraries could afford to produce a catalogue, and then largely as a one-off event. But inevitably competition forced others to follow and the increasing frequency of their publication led to a proliferation of them in the market.

A major reason for this growth stems from the way many major international photo libraries link up with each other to bolster their markets. Thus a British photo library may not only issue a catalogue of its own best selling pictures, but it may also distribute overseas libraries' catalogues over-printed with the host library's name. Can you wonder at buyers' bewilderment! They are utterly spoilt for choice.

But already newer developments have begun to rival the primacy of the printed catalogue. CD-ROMs and Internet websites are increasingly being used as a substitute for traditional catalogues, though they are not a panacea. They may be easier and cheaper to produce, and CDs more compact to store, but they still require time in searching for images that may, or may not, meet the clients' requirements.

There is already some evidence that time spent scrutinising computer screens is not particularly popular with some end users. My research suggests that some clients positively hate screen searching for images. So, there is the human factor to consider.

But the increasing competition over the past decade has largely arisen from the continuing growth in the sheer number of photo libraries. While some former specialists have diversified and grown, becoming more general in nature, their place has been taken by ever more narrowly specialised libraries.

While far from being an accurate total measure, it is interesting to see how BAPLA's membership has grown. In 1988 they had less than 200 members. Ten years later the Association's membership had reached over 350 and it is still growing rapidly, despite the occasional amalgamation of libraries via takeovers etc.

It is probably fair to assume that more photographers than ever are seeking a share of the market. Recognition of this factor should temper over-ambitious expectations of likely returns if you are a newcomer to this marketplace.

What this book covers

My previous book on this subject (*Photo Libraries & Agencies*, BFP Books, 1990) was designed to be an enduring guide to running or contributing to a photo library. Unsurprisingly, most of its principles still apply; it is the character of the marketplace which has changed.

However, after some thought and consultation, rather than just updating that earlier edition it was decided to fully revise the structure and content with the aim of strengthening the book's value, particularly to photographers seeking rewarding avenues for their freelance work.

The heart of the book comprises five chapters which address particular aspects of the subject.

Chapter 1 deals with the basic question: "What are photo libraries?". It reviews the different types of library and the essential elements of the library business.

Chapter 2 goes on to examine how libraries actually operate on a day-to-day basis. This information is essential background for photographers regardless of whether they are considering marketing their pictures directly through their own library, or indirectly through a third party.

Chapter 3 examines the range of available markets for stock photographs and addresses five different sectors:

Books;
Magazines and periodicals;
Calendars, greetings cards etc;
Advertising;
Public relations.

This arbitrary division is far from being totally inclusive but it does cover what, for many photo libraries, are the main market sectors. There are inevitable overlaps. For example, graphic designers are key customers, but they work across the board and can be found in each of the chosen sectors.

Chapter 4 on choosing a library will probably be the first to be read by many. How do you select a photo library from the hundreds of possibilities? It is a vexed question which causes many photographers problems.

The best-known library names seem to be a natural magnet for aspiring contributors, yet they are probably the most difficult to join. Why? Well it is quite simple. They already have many excellent photographers on their books and most subjects are already well covered, leaving few gaps for newcomers to fill. So this chapter will try to define a way through the jungle and save novices time through targeting libraries which offer better prospects.

Chapter 5 looks at the alternative route: how to run your own library. In other words, how to run your own small business! Many commercial photo libraries started this way, building on the nucleus of a single

Deep blue pool and sub-tropical vegetation at the Grand   **David Askham**
Hyatt Hotel, Bali. Classic stock shot capturing the appeal
of long-haul travel.

photographer's picture stock and expanding as success generated the need for new expertise and wider or deeper subject coverage.

Chapter 6 concentrates on the photographer's role, which is vitally important information regardless of which policy you adopt.

It is difficult for novices to measure their photographic skills against the high standards demanded by commercial photo libraries. While much can be learned by studying reproductions of stock photographs in print, they do not always reveal the whole story. Original colour transparencies may have been used after being cropped selectively, or overprinted with text or other graphical elements.

By far the best way is to examine – critically – original pictures which are held in a photo library and which have sold. Judge for yourself the colour quality, composition and subject choice. But of course that option may prove difficult unless you are actively negotiating a contract with a photo library.

A practical alternative is to consult the Bureau of Freelance Photographers which provides help in many fields, including a correspondence course designed to help photographers achieve the requisite standards along with a positive freelancing mentality.

In any event, this final chapter is essential reading for the novice freelance.

The reference sections at the back of the book include a review of the important role and function of BAPLA and a more detailed analysis of the impact of computerisation on the administration of modern photo libraries, as well as a glossary of terms and some useful addresses.

Finally, to give some light relief and inspiration to readers, several profiles of photographers and picture libraries are included. Reader feedback shows that profiles of this nature provide a much appreciated insight into how other people work and help to inspire newer entrants into this exciting field.

In researching these profiles, an attempt has been made to include a variety of subjects so as to provide a fair representation of successful photographers and photo libraries in operation today. The temptation to include only '"giants" has been resisted because I believe that they may not be the most promising outlets for novices to target. This judgment has been based on feedback received during my research.

So, let us move on and examine that fundamental question – what exactly are photo libraries?

1. Defining Photo Libraries

So what are photo libraries? Well, a full answer to this question may not be as simple as you think.

A novice might reply that a photo library is simply "...a repository for commercially valuable photographs waiting for customers to hire them". Another may suggest that a library is merely "...the hub of a picture marketing operation". Both replies contain an element of truth, but fall well short of a comprehensive picture.

A photo library might then be more comprehensively defined as "...a growing collection of high quality photographs, neatly captioned and efficiently administered, as well as a keenly focused marketing operation, successfully and profitably selling reproduction rights of those photographs to highly selective buyers."

But it does not end there; a prospective contributor needs to know much more in order to appreciate how the business really works. Without a fairly detailed knowledge of how photo libraries operate, a future contributing photographer is at a distinct disadvantage and is really working in the dark. In-depth information is essential.

LOOKING AT LIBRARIES

Just consider the intense competition which currently prevails, both in the market itself and among freelance photographers aspiring to be part of the action. Misdirected attempts to find an appropriate photo library with which to work, perhaps for several years, are fraught with risks. It is little wonder that the success rate may appear to be as poor as winning the national lottery.

But you can shorten the odds by developing a more in-depth understanding of the photo library business. In so doing, a photographer is

Wildlife has probably generated a greater number of specialist libraries than any other subject.

ARDEA
Wildlife and Pets
35 Brodrick Road, Wandsworth Common, London SW17 7DX
Tel: 0181 672 2067 Fax: 0181 672 8787
Email: ardea@ardea.co.uk

much more likely to make a success of selling reproduction rights of their choice stock and continuing to do so successfully over a period of years.

So the aim of this chapter is to examine and analyse the different kinds of photo libraries and then discuss how they are constituted and operate. Profiles of well-established photo libraries will help to give life to the bare organisational facts.

However you define them, the essential fact is that the description "photo libraries" covers a range of highly specialised small, medium and big businesses. Their success is measured in the revenue they can generate and the profit they make from marketing photographs supplied by individual contributing photographers.

There are several ways of categorising photo libraries. They can be considered by size – the numbers of photographs they hold or the staff they employ to run them. Given the necessary financial information (though this is rarely obtainable to make meaningful comparisons) it should also be possible to classify libraries by the size of their annual turnover in fees received.

But size is not the only, nor the principal, consideration. Many libraries are quite small businesses which are run by their original founder-owners, usually highly experienced photographers. These libraries seldom have aspirations to grow very big and not all of them represent other photographers. They can, however, be ideal models for newcomers to the field to emulate in their methods of operation.

Size is just one criterion for differentiating between different types of photo library, but it is not a particularly meaningful one.

Another way of looking at the wide variety of photo libraries throughout the world today would be to comprehensively review the whole range of subjects which they represent. Done successfully, the result would be an encyclopaedic tome of undoubted value, but well beyond the declared scope of this book. It would also need very regular updating if it was to remain of value, and that would be economically unviable.

The primary method used in this book is to simply divide photo libraries into two groups: those which claim to be general libraries and those which choose to specialise in a limited range of subjects.

There is a very good reason for adopting this method of classifying photo libraries. Most photographers, whether professional or part-time freelances, already have their own clearly identifiable specialisations. It therefore simplifies the selection process if photographers recognise themselves as either specialists or generalists and research outlets in the appropriate sectors.

Let us start with a review of specialist libraries and the process by which they are established. Then we will see why they are so popular and successful.

The public's insatiable demand for celebrity photographs has spawned many specialist agencies covering this lucrative field.

Specialist libraries

Many photographers operate in clearly defined fields, usually linked either to their clients' special requirements or their own personal inclinations and expertise – though many may have long forgotten how they became specialists!

For example, a photographer may excel at photographing home interiors, possibly working with qualified stylists who furnish and dress rooms to achieve specific illusions or results. After a few years, such a photographer could have produced and retained the copyright to many thousands of photographs of interiors, many of which could be reused in the future for illustrative or advertising purposes (subject to obtaining any necessary releases of course). Such a collection could form the natural nucleus of a new photo library.

You might think that the range of subjects which could legitimately be considered as suitable for a specialist library would be infinite. Taken to extremes, almost any noun – even abstract ones – listed in an English dictionary could become a specialist subject, much like the range of esoteric subjects once chosen by BBC Mastermind contestants. Multiply that number by any number of other countries and you have a new dimension of potential subjects.

In practice, the range of subjects depends upon the degree of specialisation. For example, many so-called travel libraries were launched in the belief that "travel" would be a lucrative market sector. But travel is "a journey through or across an area, region, country or continent, terminating at one or more destinations." Each of these areas, regions and destinations could each be treated as different specialist photographic subjects, as indeed, could be the means of travelling and the peoples encountered en route.

You can see how easily it becomes quite complex to define "travel" when you probe more deeply. You can also see why travel photo libraries in particular have diversified over the years, as their sub-specialisations and filing cabinets grew.

While, in theory, there are almost unlimited numbers of specialist subjects, the same cannot be said of matching markets. You may be the world's leading expert on integrated circuits or domestic fleas, but continuing demand for photographs of these subjects may be extremely limited. You may struggle to make a living out of your obscure specialisation. On the other hand, as a successful photographer of people displaying human emotions, you may well have the makings of a specialism greatly in demand.

One has to be realistic. In the main you will be supplying and negotiating with a buyer's market. Unless you have hard evidence that there is a real market for your special subject (more about this aspect in a later chapter), then you would be unwise to invest time and money in the hope of creating such a market.

General libraries

After briefly reviewing the nature of specialist photo libraries, we are well on the way to gaining an understanding of general libraries.

It would be tempting to assume that a general photo library is a blend of disparate specialist picture collections. In some cases, that assumption may be true. It depends how those libraries started in business and were later developed; no two businesses evolve in an equal or preordained fashion. But generally one finds unifying themes running through general photo libraries' collections.

Not surprisingly, many general libraries started life as specialists. As their collections grew, so the number of sub-divisions increased and diversified, though usually the subsections bore some family resemblance to the core subjects.

For example, a travel library may have been launched as a specialist collection of pictures of England, then later expanded to encompass the whole of the United Kingdom. Later still, overseas travel may have extended the coverage into Europe and beyond so that it became a truly global collection. By that stage it is likely that many contributing photographers would have been recruited to help keep the library's material up-to-date.

At that phase of its evolution it might be thought that it was still a specialist travel library; but the odds are that it had already diversified to make use of non-travel pictures which had been acquired by contributing photographers as a by-product of their travel. Industry, transportation, architecture, food, lifestyle – all of these are examples of important subjects which will be photographed by the innovative and flexible specialist travel photographer.

Some general photo libraries have grown in leaps and bounds by acquiring specialist photographic collections which supplement, rather than conflict with, the subjects already held in stock. Those collections often came from experienced photographers who had reached retirement age or were changing direction in their professional lives. Some of those photographers may well continue to supply new material to the library, whereas others make a complete break.

Work of the latter group will, inevitably, assume historical overtones.

Seasonal images of the English countryside have many uses as stock shots, including meeting the needs of calendar and other publishers.   **Collections/John D Beldom**

But that is not necessarily a negative quality. For growing photo libraries, the acquisition of historic material adds a valuable time dimension to their stock. And not all such stock becomes dated; sometimes it possesses timeless, even artistic, qualities. Such material has real value over time.

Whatever the situation, the new additions will – if their judgment is

Including a person in the shot adds saleability, not only by helping to show the scale of a famous feature but by adding life and colour to what might otherwise be a very static and monochrome subject.

**Collections/
Michael Diggin**

sound – complement the acquiring library's stock.

In other cases, photo libraries expand by merging their businesses. A travel library once boasted that it had taken ten years to build up one million images – and one day to add the second million! The explanation was that it had acquired a travel company's own picture library. But of course the value of that new accession would have diminished fairly quickly without a carefully planned updating of the acquired stock.

OPERATIONAL FACTORS

It is most important for would-be contributing photographers, or those aiming to operate their own small library, to understand how professional photo libraries are run on a day-to-day basis. But it also worth considering their reasons for running in the first place and the financial criteria that make these businesses sustainable.

25

Business basics

With a few exceptions, most photo libraries are operated as stand-alone small businesses. The exceptions tend to be multinational organisations with a global network, or small information sections which form part of the public relations departments of big companies or governmental bodies. Some international news agencies also fall into this category. By any calculations, they are big businesses.

Naturally, to succeed, photo libraries have to remain financially sound and make an acceptable profit, year after year. Without profit a business would soon become unsustainable and certainly would not be able to invest in new equipment – essential in order to keep pace with advancing information and administrative technology.

Just consider the inroads made by personal computers, bar-code readers, electronic databases and computerised accounting during the past decade. Any photo library which is inclined to ignore such tools for progress clearly risks falling behind and its business may soon decline.

Apart from these essential operational aspects, photo libraries require suitable accommodation, competent staff, effective organisation and productive and efficient procedures. All these too require financing.

To a keen photographer, whose first priority is getting out and producing new photographs, these essential library administrative matters must sound extremely boring. But for a productive library, good administration is crucial to success.

Location

Location is an important factor, mainly in relation to accessibility to the major markets, though this was a more important consideration a few years ago than it is today. Then, it was vital to be near the picture researchers and publishers who regularly patronised your library. Usually this meant setting up business in the major cities, principally London, where of course you still find many of the longer-established photo libraries.

Two factors have impacted on the former situation. First, communications have changed beyond the wildest dreams of business people a decade or two ago, with photographs being transmitted globally in near real time. Pictures acquired on location can be incorporated into newspapers within minutes of being taken, having been digitised and transmitted in unbelievably short times; imagine how much easier it is for this sort of operation to be launched from a well-equipped modern office.

The point has been reached when original colour transparencies

People are an essential element in much travel stock photography. Well considered images of local characters often evoke a sense of place better than any simple view.

Collections/Alain Le Garsmeur

need never leave their photo libraries. Thumb-nail versions of short-listed pictures can be transmitted to the client, either on CD-ROMs or directly by satellite, radio or landline telecommunications. Full versions of any chosen images can then be delivered in the same way.

The second factor which has changed is the relocation of many publishers outside the metropolis. Clients are more widely scattered, not only in the United Kingdom but globally. International clients are now more readily reached by modern telecommunications, thus negating the need to set up allied offices on other continents.

On balance, these days a new photo library could set up almost anywhere, provided it accepts the need for state-of-the-art telecommunications and recognises that the more remote its location, the less likely it is to receive visits from picture researchers. That may or may not be important.

Clients and marketing

In order for libraries to remain financially sound and continue to make a profit, they have to research and develop a responsive and rewarding

The usual insistence on cloudless blue skies may not apply where the subject lends itself to a dramatic or atmospheric interpretation.

**Collections/
Roy Stedall-Humphryes**

client base. Therefore library managers have to acquire effective marketing skills and devote time, on a continuing basis, to building up a good portfolio of customers.

All income is derived from fees charged to clients for the loan and use of pictures held in the library. The nature of the usage and associated reproduction rights required by the client are important factors which have to be spelled out clearly, because they have a marked influence on the fees negotiated. For example, a photograph used nationally on giant advertising hoardings would earn many times the fee obtained if the same picture was used as a tiny image on a product label, or as a small reproduction in a consumer magazine.

To assist picture researchers, libraries usually have their own standard scale of fees covering the most typical contracts with their clients, though inevitably circumstances frequently dictate the need for negotiation.

Sometimes big publishers expect a discount, particularly if they wish to negotiate the use of an agreed number of the library's pictures in a year. It is in an area like this that effective interpersonal and negotiating skills are needed if the library business is to prosper.

Maintaining stock

After the above overview of financial issues we should now consider the most important factor of all: the stock of pictures themselves.

In order to be commercially attractive to picture researchers and other clients a photo library must have a reasonably comprehensive collection of photographs in stock and readily available for loan. Each subject area needs to be as sensibly complete as possible, otherwise picture researchers will soon learn that it is a waste of time contacting that particular library.

There is a fundamental requirement, therefore, for the photo library owner or manager to scrutinise the stock of pictures, anticipate future requirements, fill any gaps, and keep the stock up-to-date. As part of this process, good managers make sure that their most responsive contributing photographers are regularly issued with "Wants Lists" detailing subjects currently being sought.

Occasionally, in order to fill important gaps, managers will commission photography, either from photographers on their staff, or from freelance photographers expert in that particular field.

Reaching clients

The final aspect of handling picture stock is the process whereby selected material has to be despatched to potential clients.

In most cases – certainly at the time of writing – photographs are still physically loaned to clients for an agreed period of time and for a clearly defined usage. This process is called physical transmission and involves the pictures leaving the library temporarily.

Pictures have to be packaged safely, accounted for, and sent by post or courier. Then when the photographs are returned, library staff have to check their condition, book them back into the library, re-file them for future use and invoice the client.

However this method of delivery is already changing as advantageous electronic systems become economically viable and grow in popularity. In contrast to physical transmission, new digital technology leaves the original photographs intact in the library. Instead of valuable originals, digitised copies of photographs can be sent to clients for use in accordance with the library's usual terms of business.

Some photo libraries specialise in actually selling CD-ROMs containing themed images for use free from royalty payments. This somewhat controversial practice will be studied in more detail later in the book.

Despite the advances and changes touched on above, most libraries continue to operate using more traditional methods.

SUMMARY

The aim of this chapter has been to build up a more accurate picture of what photo libraries actually are and how they operate. We have looked at the different types of photo library and taken the lid off their organisation, their resources and the way they go about their business.

Photographers have been given a first insight into the nature of a relationship with a library and received the first clues as to whether to contribute or consider running their own. But many of these factors will be examined again – certainly in more detail – once we have examined the potential markets for stock photographs in the next chapter.

Profile

Collections

Collections was the brainchild of photographer Brian Shuel, and has developed in a big way since it was launched in 1990.

With the help of his wife Sal, Brian had been marketing his own specialist collections of "British Customs" and "Bridges" (plus other by-products of his work as a professional photographer) since about 1975. Then they decided, for several good reasons, to further develop this side of his business.

Brian explains: "Our idea was to take on other substantial collec-

Brian Shuel at work in the Collections office.　　　　**John Tracy**

Guy Fawkes bonfire – one of Brian Shuel's own best-selling images which is in demand every year as November 5th comes around.

Collections/Brian Shuel

Stone lion on Westminster Bridge, London. As well as an **Collections/Robert Hallman**
excellent shot of the subject itself, this could find many uses as
an image of British Empire.

tions of photographs, of a similar comprehensive nature, in the hope that it would develop into a sort of general photo library of the British Isles. Each photographer would have sole rights to his or her own subject, so that there would be minimal competition within the library. Hence the name Collections.

"The reasons for confining stock to the British Isles were both physical and mental: we never wanted to get too big, and we knew our area very well.

"Unfortunately, it didn't work out as we expected! We did get a few collections but, on the whole, the best individual collections were already running very successfully in the hands of their creators. And sadly, many of the collections we were offered were by experts who were extremely knowledgeable about their subjects but who lacked photo-graphic expertise. So we moved to 'Plan B'.

"We solicited topographical area collections, rather than subject collections. This plan worked better, but there were still problems; most contributing photographers simply failed to do what they said they would. Many thought that their own home areas were boring and wanted to photograph anywhere else rather than their local subjects.

"So 'Plan C' evolved. We still encouraged contributors to specialise, but eventually we decided to consider any other UK pictures they wanted to submit.

"Now we have an amazing coverage of England and excellent files on Wales and Ireland. Only Scotland remains a problem. In addition, we have separate sections including industry, religions, events, abstracts and emergency services. Many of the original subject collections – castles, bridges, trains and canals – have been integrated into the county files. My British Customs collection remains intact – though augmented by many other contributors – and is by far the most comprehensive of its type anywhere.

"Family Life exists as almost a separate library within Collections and covers pregnancy, birth, babies, child development, education etc. The core collection was supplied by Anthea Sieveking and is now supplied by a few specialist professionals who know all of the problems involved."

In 1999 the library held around 500,000 pictures supplied by some 150 contributing photographers. Turnover is about 20 times what it was ten years ago and Brian reckons he obtains a good deal more revenue from his 50% share of income from his British Customs pictures than he did in 1989 when he retained 100% of the fees they earned. Clearly there is a lesson here, showing that a library needs to grow beyond its lower critical mass.

Like many small photo libraries, Collections is a family-run business. Brian and Sal were the original partners. though daughter-in-law Laura Boswell and elder son Simon Shuel were also there from the beginning.

Laura, now a partner, is "a whizz on the financial side", which becomes increasingly important as the business grows, while Simon – a graphic designer by trade – is an expert computer programmer. He looks after the library's seven personal computers, writes all of the application programmes and designs all of the publicity material, including their web-site. This is a classic conjunction of complementary skills which works very well. Temporary staff are hired as needed.

What of the future? Brian tries to sketch out the options.

"We are debating our future on many fronts: ourselves, the house, the contributors, the marketplace, the stock, the competition, electronics.

"Let's start with accommodation. Collections grew up in our house, but currently the library wins by four rooms to three. We would like our house back! But if we consider moving to new accommodation, apart from the financial costs and inevitable disruption, there is a distinct risk that we might lose the very friendly atmosphere which our customers like.

"Then there is the question of increasing competition. To be successful we have to become better and better and we have to offer material that isn't available elsewhere. Many of our images are unique and it would be self-destructive to promote them in catalogues or as clip-art. The fact is that we have a vast knowledge of our subject and have access to literally thousands of books and other reference material which you simply cannot buy from CDs or library catalogues.

"Many picture researchers and editors hate on-line and CD-ROM searching because it is painfully slow and impossible to discuss with third parties. That is a strong reason, I believe, why our customers come to us."

With such a dichotomy between satisfying success and difficult future decisions, I asked Brian Shuel what advice he would give to any photographer contemplating launching a new photo library into the currently highly saturated and competitive world?

"If you mull over building a vast international library and becoming a millionaire, forget it. It takes years and the competition is ferocious. Even after fifty years of the modern photo library business, there are very few owners driving around in the latest BMW, let alone a Rolls Royce.

"A lone photographer can supplement his income handsomely, provided the stock is either good enough to be sought after by name (we have only six photographers in this category), or is of subjects which people want but can't get anywhere else.

"Once you take on other photographers you have to decide either to run the library yourself – to the probable detriment of your photographic time – or take on staff which adds to the overheads and management demands. It took us five years to attain our initial turnover target. Not everyone has the patience, knowledge or faith."

Seldom has a founding partner of a small photo library been so open and honest about the challenging business of running a library in an era of tremendous technological and commercial change.

2.

How Libraries Work

From a general overview of what libraries are, the markets they supply, and their place in the picture marketing chain, we now move on to a more detailed examination of their day-to-day operations.

From what has been reviewed so far, it must be apparent that like all businesses photo libraries require efficient organisation if they are to meet their objectives. There are many aspects to good organisation, so first we will outline the essentials and then examine them in more detail.

BASIC ORGANISATION

To begin at the beginning, where would you expect to find pictures libraries?

The ideal location for any photo library would be near to the majority of their target customers. So unsurprisingly you find a concentration of such businesses in and around the major cities. But here, unfortunately, property prices and rents are higher than in the provinces, and this can prove prohibitive.

However, many specialist photo libraries succeed despite being fairly inaccessible to visiting picture researchers. Indeed, one of the profiles in this book features a small library located in remote Orkney!

The location of photo libraries does have a marked influence on their internal organisation. A library which is frequently visited by picture researchers needs to be organised in such a way that the researchers have a suitably furnished area, equipped with large light boxes, to facilitate picture selection. It needs to be user-friendly.

Such facilities would not be required by a photo library located in a rural area which is seldom visited by clients.

The basic components of any photo library include a picture storage

A stock image lifted out of the ordinary by the fortuitous appearance of a flock of seagulls.

Collections/Mike Kipling

system, viewing tables for picture selection whether by staff or visiting picture researchers, a despatch and receipt section, and an administrative section. The size and complexity of these sections should be related to the size of the individual photo library business and the nature of their transactions.

In addition, as with any type of workplace, there is also a need for toilet, washroom and light catering facilities, plus storage space for consumables.

Finally, no business today can manage without telecommunications of one kind or another.

Storage systems

The most crucial aspect of photographic stock-keeping is that original photographs are valuable – often irreplaceable – and have to be stored somewhere secure yet accessible. No longer are recycled shoe boxes acceptable!

Gone too are the days when any old filing cabinet or chest of drawers could be adapted to store pictures, although simple suspension files can be effective, particularly when related sets of photographs need to be stored together.

Some photo agencies specialise in commissioning and marketing complete picture stories which can be leased in their entirety and syndicated worldwide. There is thus no point in breaking down such a series to fit into a different system of filing. If necessary, key pictures can be duplicated and filed in specialist sections.

There are various forms of proprietary storage cabinets suitable for the purpose, some with shallow drawers ready to take standard mounted and masked photographs and others which accept specially designed suspension files which are ideal for filing groups of transparencies.

A well-organised photo library manager will have thought about future growth and will have settled on a solution which ensures matching storage units of uniform height.

If a library is likely to attract a fair number of visiting picture researchers, life can be made easier for them if a representative selection of the most successful pictures – or master copies if duplicates have been produced – are stored in such a way that they can brought swiftly into a good viewing position. At the very least there should be large area with high-quality illuminated viewing tables set aside exclusively for this purpose.

One successful specialist photo library has a system of parallel rails installed inside a large bespoke viewing cabinet in such a way that selected suspended sheets of pocketed colour transparencies can be glided into a back-illuminated viewing position. If alternative images are needed, it is a simple matter to check the sample images' reference numbers and retrieve other related pictures from more conventional storage systems, usually tailor-made compartmented drawers.

An essential adjunct to picture storage systems is an efficient, uncomplicated search and retrieval system.

In the early days, the most successful libraries depended on staff with extremely good memories – human computers! But as stock grew, staff changed and new technology promised easier solutions, photo libraries have become increasingly dependent on computerised stock control and accounting systems.

Computers and communications

Only a few decades ago the average photo library simply needed office space, staff, a telephone and a typewriter in order to conduct its business. The Royal Mail handled most deliveries of pictures to and from clients, or picture researchers visited the library and collected selected images.

Compare that snapshot view with the situation today. Computers have replaced typewriters and accounting ledgers; facsimile transmission and electronic mail (e-mail) have added a new dimension to communications; courier services have siphoned off much business formerly handled by the Post Office, and CD-ROMs have made possible new ways of marketing and supplying visual images to clients.

Even in 1988 when I was researching my first book on this subject, few photo libraries had invested in desktop computing for administration or accounting. Now a photo library would be behind the times and certainly less efficient than the competition without embracing such technology.

It is a similar story regarding digital imaging and the Internet. Correspondence by e-mail was not even a gleam in the eye a few years ago; now the bigger libraries conduct a significant amount of their business through the World Wide Web or Internet. Digitisation of images has also become a feature of bigger libraries.

Already some leading photo libraries have reported that their marketing through the Internet has reached new and hitherto unknown clients around the world. Communication has been established through e-mail with images transmitted electronically, leaving the original colour transparencies safe in the host library.

It is clear that businesses have to keep abreast of new developments and make value judgments on whether to invest and when, and there is no doubt that new technology is beginning to transform how many libraries work in a quite radical way. As a consequence, photo library organisation has to take into account the technical hardware and the space and utility services required by these new systems and facilities.

STOCK MANAGEMENT

There are two essential aspects of stock management, one internal and the other external.

Internal management

Internal stock management probably consumes most time because there are so many facets. Stock is built up after careful editing of raw submissions or newly generated material, then processing them into the stan-

Gilded figure in the Royal Palace, Bangkok, symbolising the artistic culture and heritage of the Thai capital. Such details are often sought to add interest to travel features.

David Askham

dard format for the library. Pictures need to be filed in specified locations so that retrieval can be swiftly executed.

While there is a certain frisson of excitement in assembling pictures

Persian cat, shot in the studio. The market may often require formal shots **David Askham**
such as this to clearly illustrate breed characteristics, although "action"
shots may also be required.

from the library and despatching them to clients with genuine optimism that they will be used and earn reproduction fees, eventually they will be returned to the library. What happens then?

All too often their inward processing through the accounting system, checking for damage or necessary re-sleeving, calling the clients to account for discrepancies, and re-filing stock, is seen as a low-priority chore. The author has seen tables laden with returned packages or heaps of pictures waiting to be filed, and wondered whether such oversight reflected the general standard of that library's internal administration.

Dealing with returns should be dealt with as expeditiously as despatches, allocating a member of staff specifically to process such pictures.

Managing stock pictures also entails a regular conscious review of existing stock, extracting pictures which have aged or deteriorated or patently will never sell, and commissioning new photography to update and enlarge the sections covered by the library. This act of good husbandry is frequently given a lower priority than it deserves, but is something that should be scheduled for regular action, purging stock at least annually.

External management

External stock management may seem to be a contradiction in terms; once pictures have been despatched to clients there would seem to be little the library can do.

Wrong! Pictures will have been sent out with a covering despatch note containing details of return dates. Part of a library's management responsibility is to keep a check on "dues in" and when necessary actively progress their return. Otherwise stock will languish with publishers and run a greater risk of loss or damage. Perhaps even more important, the library is being denied the opportunity of re-marketing them to other clients.

Despite the best safeguards, from time-to-time pictures will go astray and be lost or destroyed – sometimes by sheer accident, sometimes through sheer incompetence.

Many years ago, some of my irreplaceable photographs of rare aircraft were inadvertently fed into the office shredder by an inexperienced member of a client's staff. Compensation was ultimately paid, but the blunder soured the relationship.

A photo library should first take all precautions to prevent loss within the library, or while pictures are in transit. This comes down to careful administration.

Packages can be insured to cover delivery, but once in the clients' hands it is they who must accept responsibility for safe custody. But in the event of loss or damage, there should be no dispute about the level of compensation provided the terms of delivery spell out the contractual obligations of the client.

The need for new material

This subject was introduced in the previous section but is worthy of a little expansion here.

Some years ago, before the rapid expansion of modern photo

libraries, a library founding partner spent some time, every month, sending out for publication a "Wants List" of subjects she felt would be useful in the library. As one of her specialisations was worldwide travel, she systematically studied a world atlas and listed all the significant towns, cities and places of tourist interest in specific countries.

As a result she attracted new photographers who worked assiduously meeting her requirements. Often there was no immediate need, but she knew that one day many pictures drawn from this exercise would be of value. And she was right. Her foresight generated an enviable income for the library over several years.

A few decades have passed, competition has grown, and the world has effectively shrunk as travel times diminish and more and more photographers scour the world for new pictures. Clients now insist on recent coverage of classic global destinations. So there is now an increasing need to re-shoot topographical material to reflect architectural changes, modernised skylines and people's evolving fashions in clothes and consumer goods. The world is a far from static place and changes ever faster.

No one library can keep up with this enormous evolving demand, which is good news for the industry at large. But each library possessing enterprise and vision will be giving thought to future needs and making sure that its photographers are aware of those needs.

Sometimes a library may need to seek new photographers who are capable of shooting new material, perhaps with a characteristic style. Even the small photo library run by one photographer should not spurn the idea of recruiting help, possibly in areas beyond their usual specialisation or availability to shoot. After all, any one-person library inevitably has their time diluted by having to run the business as well as shooting new stock.

In summary, if a library relies only on the routine input of the owner/photographer, or of an unchanging group of contributing photographers under contract, it may be missing lucrative marketing opportunities. All should consciously devote time, periodically, to planning new photography acquisitions.

PEOPLE AND PROCEDURES

Probably the most priceless asset possessed by well-run photo libraries are the people who make the whole operation work. At the same time, the smooth and efficient running of a photo library often depends on the staff consistently following set procedures.

Staff

It is too easy for them to be taken for granted, but there is no doubt that the success of the best libraries is a reflection of the leadership, the management, and the calibre of the people involved. The difference between an intelligent and a casual approach to interpreting a client's picture requirements or skilfully negotiating fees, can be measured in the sales achieved.

Probably the number one reason given by contributing photographers for changing photo libraries is that something is lacking in the library's performance. However, this is an over-simplification of a controversial issue which will be addressed in a later chapter. Faults can often lie with contributing photographers.

Where staff numbers justify it, a mixture of skills can be found. Cataloguing new pictures can be a boring and repetitive process and requires a temperament unruffled by such work. In contrast, staff involved with internal picture research to satisfy external clients' needs require discerning judgement of good picture quality, the ability to think laterally ("Send me a picture of a yellow flower!"), wide general knowledge and good inter-personal skills.

No amount of college training is likely to produce ideal candidates. So the better libraries recognise the need for internal and on-the-job training. Their results show, though training is often difficult to dovetail into a frantic daily routine.

Trainee library personnel seldom have detailed insight into the way pictures are integrated into newspapers, magazines, books or advertising. Yet such knowledge can be invaluable to them when they are selecting a small number of pictures from possibly thousands of the subject in stock.

Brief visits, or even short-term secondment, into a clients' working environment can be beneficial. Sometimes photo library staff are deliberately recruited from the sharp end of the publishing industry and they, in turn, can help train their photo library colleagues. Equally it is not uncommon for external picture researchers to find employment in photo libraries in order to broaden their own professional knowledge. Both parties can benefit.

Staff continuity is important. Clients become used to dealing with specific photo library staff members and both parties benefit from the good relationships and understanding built up over time. Inspired staff selection and humane and generous treatment help to keep a happy team intact and the library profitable.

Contributing photographers also gain when photo library staff

Autumn colours, a useful stock image for evoking the season, but also abstract enough for a range of graphic design uses.

David Askham

remain unchanged. It takes time for a library picture researcher and a photographer to understand each other's needs and capabilities. Both suffer when the process has to begin all over again.

Procedures

Visiting a library some years ago, I witnessed a mountainous pile of packages of photographs returned by clients. On a subsequent visit, they were still there; still waiting to be unpacked, checked for use or damage, remounted if necessary and re-filed in their storage cabinets.

Just imagine the potential loss of future earnings from that material, the delay in chasing payments, or investigating and charging for any damage to the photographs. It was left to the over-worked manager to handle returns, but there were no procedures for delegating this work and supervising its completion.

It may sound unnecessarily bureaucratic to advocate the drafting of key procedures to cover the various recurring activities in a photo library's administration. But problems start when a small library, which is quite capable of handling the comparatively low turnover of stock in the beginning, expands and takes on additional staff. It only takes some staff leave, sickness or other unpredictable distractions to show the weaknesses in any organisation. If new or temporary staff arrive to help out and there are no written procedures to help them understand the way the library works, delays and problems accumulate.

Simple written procedures are an invaluable training aid for new or temporary members of staff and thoroughly deserve consideration by library managers. They will gain from both reduced questioning by uncertain staff and greater efficiency in the business.

New technology poses a threat to some people who may think that their jobs are at risk. Maybe the operation of a new computer system has to be learned. But how much easier it is for staff if they can follow logical procedures evolved by an expert, be it someone from the library or the supplier.

They may be thought of as a distraction, but drafting procedures must be seen as a positive contribution to the smooth operation of a business.

LIBRARIES AND PHOTOGRAPHERS

It is important to examine libraries' relationships with their contributing photographers, a relationship of importance equal to that between a library and its clients.

Photographers represent the vital supply side of the photo library business; without a continuing injection of new photographs, a library's turnover would soon suffer.

Managing photographers

The expression "managing photographers" may sound like an overstatement, even heavy-handed. However, most contributing photographers would not recognise that they were being managed, yet would certainly not object to the idea that their photographs were being managed by the library.

Some libraries develop a more active relationship with their photographers than do others. It is a two-way process. Photographers who send off a batch of new pictures only once in a while and seldom liaise with their library, probably do not deserve the rewards obtained by those who make a point of eliciting a library's current requirements and making regular new contributions.

An active, dynamic library manager will keep an eye on his or her contributors, offering encouragement when it is needed and praise when appropriate. This managerial approach is important and should be identified before a commitment to a library is made.

Good photo libraries make a point of issuing, from to time to time, lists of subjects which they have been unable to supply to clients from their existing stock. Good contributing photographers make a point of responding to these lists, thereby helping to build up profitable relationships with the library. Sometimes library picture researchers will telephone specific contributing photographers and suggest that they try to cover subjects known to be in demand. From personal experience I know that this happens.

One cold winter's morning, I received a telephone call pleading that I try and photograph hoar frost on winter berries. I may not have been the only one approached; however, I stopped what I was doing, spent an hour in freezing weather shooting the subject required, and submitted the results as soon as possible.

Those pictures were well received and have been consistently good seasonal sellers ever since. I doubt that I would have received that call had I been a dormant contributor. So the moral is clear: show willing and a library manager is more likely to suggest potentially saleable subjects.

Contracts and fees

When a new contributing photographer joins a photo library it is common practice for a contract to be drawn up spelling out the terms.

The terms will vary from one library to another, but generally they will cover the minimum period that a photographer's pictures will be retained, the way in which new material should be submitted, the allocation and payment of fees, and any exclusivity conditions.

Most libraries divide the fees they receive 50/50 – half remains with the library and half is paid to the photographer. There are some varia-

Elaborate decorations destined for hotel guests' tables in Bali. **David Askham**
Such attractive details are useful in conveying the different
cultural characteristics of foreign lands.

tions to this rule, usually resulting from the imposition of further commission payments to overseas agents who may have been brought into

the selling chain. In those cases, the photographer receives rather less than half the original fee.

It is not uncommon for new contributing photographers to be critical of the fact that libraries retain so much as half of the fees received. But in order to achieve their level of success, they must set up and operate costly businesses, all of which must be funded by the generated income. Nevertheless it is this fact, more than any other, which prompts many would-be contributors to set up their own libraries so as to avoid this apparent loss of income.

That is their choice and one that we shall look at more closely in a later chapter. But for the moment, try to accept that without photo libraries' wider marketing expertise and client base a photographer's sales would, in most cases, be greatly diminished. If a library can achieve more than twice the sales return you are likely to achieve by yourself, then the economic argument is proved.

Photo libraries usually pay their contributing photographers on a quarterly basis (some more frequently), often by direct credit into a nominated account. At the same time the library will send out a statement showing what sales have been made, to whom, for what purpose, what limited rights were sold in which pictures, and the fees received. This is very useful information. It bears close scrutiny and, periodically, analysis to see how the photographer and library are performing.

Not all libraries give so much information, but now that most have computerised accounting systems there is really no excuse why reasonably comprehensive information should not be given on a regular basis.

SECURITY

The final section of this chapter addresses the vexed question of security. Security comes in many forms but, for the purpose of this book, two aspects will be considered: physical and intellectual security of images, and security of information.

All photographs have intrinsic value which is very difficult to quantify. An accountant may take the view that each photograph produced has material and allied cost components; he is unconcerned that the majority of photographs produced probably will never earn any fees at all. So the actual costs of materials, travel, and other production costs, plus a share of overheads such as insurance, camera repairs etc, descend on that small minority of saleable images.

In theory you could put a unit production cost on each picture deposited in a photo library. What happens, then, if one or more photographs are lost, especially when they were with a client?

Photo libraries publish terms of loan on their delivery notes which spell out a client's financial responsibility in the event of loss or damage. Compensation can typically run into hundreds of pounds, occasionally significantly higher, depending on certain factors.

For example, some subjects are irreplaceable. Clearly history cannot be repeated. But often a contemporary picture sells because of some transient quality, such as an atmospheric shaft of sunlight on a landscape, or an engaging human expression. How could that be repeated? Financial compensation attempts to offset the loss of potential sales in the future.

Another important aspect of physical security is the safe transmission of pictures between the photo library and clients. In most cases, depending on the perceived value of the items sent, packages are insured by one means or another. Of course digital transmission solves this problem.

Often, apparently lost pictures are not lost at all, merely misplaced. But months or years may elapse before they come to light. Who then pays for loss of potential earnings?

So physical security is a vitally important part of a photo library's operation and administration.

The second consideration is that of security of information. Few people realise that this form of security is a concern of photo libraries. To understand the risk, consider the planning and long lead times before a new book or magazine can be launched. Inevitably, photo libraries are among the first to learn about a publisher's plans.

During the planning and gestation period picture researchers are privileged to be party to confidential information; it is an essential feature of their jobs. So when they start their research there must be either a bond of trust, or veil of secrecy, over the uses to which they plan to put library pictures.

It is for this reason that security of information, or commercial integrity, call it what you will, is a vitally important quality essential to the way photo library staff go about their daily work.

Profile

Arena Images

Arena Images is a young, London-based specialist business which combines the traditional roles of a photo library with the less usual function of photographer's agent. It is a library and agency for performance pictures, centred on the arts.

It was founded in January 1998 by Rachel Hughes to fill a niche market and is run by a team of five people, including three who work part-time.

No other agency exists in the United Kingdom that specialises in arts and entertainment while acting as both a stock photo library and an agent for its contracted photographers. I asked Rachel what background skills she brought to such a specialised business.

"I studied English and Music, became a teacher, and then worked at the Arts Theatre in London. I also spent time working for Sky Photographic in their professional laboratory and as a photographic assistant. In addition I gained experience as a freelance theatre photographer and a picture researcher."

What an interesting combination of professional skills and how relevant to the business she helped to launch.

Rachel has recruited eighteen contributing photographers, from the United Kingdom and overseas. One third are female. But she also spends time talent-spotting via photographer-credited pictures in relevant publications. She also calls on a few other photographers who, while not being regular contributors, meet her special requests from time-to-time.

I asked Rachel what she expected from her new photographers.

"For stock photography, we expect a photographer to possess a significant collection of relevant images, though not necessarily a large quantity provided there is a distinctive style and the quality is good. Usually we would like to start with at least 100 pictures and expect reg-

Flamenco dancer Anna Leon, capturing the movement
and colour of the dance.

Arena Images/Hilary Shedel

ular contributions of new material.

"For agency photography, We look for photographers with well-presented portfolios, a good manner and a base in the performing arts. Specially commissioned work accounts for about 25% of new photography added to the library."

Currently the library has around 15,000 images of which approximately two-thirds are already digitised for archival and delivery purposes. Interestingly, although most pictures are shot on reversal material, many are colour negatives. The material's wider exposure latitude helps to overcome the extremes of contrasty lighting in certain performance arenas.

Although the arts sector is highly specialised, there were several well established libraries already in the field. So building up a new client base was not free from competition. Impressive marketing was the key to solving this fundamental problem. It was achieved by well drafted letters of introduction, use of advertising cards, personal visits and advertisements in relevant magazines.

Another competitive factor is the stylistic quality of many of Arena's

A striking image of circus performer Rob Horsmann,
illustrating the stylistic originality of much of Arena's stock. **Arena Images/Eric Richmond**

images, which go beyond the classic documentary genre. This subtle quality appeals particularly to advertising and design-based clients.

On the administrative side, the business was computerised from the beginning using Logic Information Systems as prime contractor. While accepting that the programmes were not designed for her particular library, Rachel is pleased with the capabilities and performance and particularly relieved that she did not have to underwrite the full software development costs.

All in-house database functions are up and running very effectively despite some problems with the accounts side of the package. Only a web-based database remains to be introduced.

Rachel added, "Electronic delivery of photographic images from the library is working well and has proved excellent for newspapers, magazines and overseas clients. It has turned out to be a very popular facility. Certainly we see the operation of an effective website as opening up new markets, particularly in the international arena."

With so much achieved in a comparatively short time, I asked Rachel whether her planned expectations had been met.

"Although we have kept to our original plans generally, we have found certain areas expanding more quickly than we expected. For example, our original intention was to develop the stock side of the business and then work on the agency side later. However, the agency work has gathered momentum faster than projected and we have had to make changes to our planned working practices and also to our financial reporting, because of the different contracts used for commissioned work.

"Our experience in this field appeals to many clients and we are already diversifying slightly so that we can provide a service which is clearly in demand. For example, several of our photographers already undertake non-arts work. So when we can see opportunities for capitalising on their particular skills, exemplified by the styles they deliver in their performing arts photography, we will definitely expand our agency service to generate more work for them."

Finally, what advice did Rachel have for a specialist photographer thinking about establishing a photo library in a new niche area?

"Research carefully the computerised database needed for a new photo library. Image digitisation should be planned for from launch, as should a website capable of selling and delivering images from the library.

"Finally, take a good long holiday beforehand; there may not be another opportunity for a long time!"

3.   Markets and Requirements

Photographers, generally speaking, are optimistic people and this mood of optimism extends to believing that there is a market for most of the photographs they produce.

Oh, if only it was that simple!

In theory they are probably right, but in practice it is a very different story. Market requirements are constantly changing, reflecting the moods of the moment and plans for the future. Editors and art directors seem to be constantly changing jobs with a frequency incomparable with the situation a few decades ago. Each new appointment heralds changes as the new incumbents try to stamp their personalities on their positions of authority.

Topical news is covered live by specialist media photographers and their work is often syndicated around the world if deemed sufficiently newsworthy. Many picture requirements in other fields, particularly in advertising and public relations, are met by specially commissioned photographers who again specialise in that type of work.

So with so much photography covered by specific commissions, where is the market for stock photography? Where are the markets?

THE MARKET FOR STOCK

Time and money are probably the most important factors which influence editors' or art directors' decisions as to whether they should commission new photography or use stock library pictures.

It is the media's constant fight against time which gives photo libraries such a keen marketing edge. If there is not time to send a photographer to some distant location, editors turn to picture libraries to see if they can solve their problems.

Spitfire in front of the Royal Air Force Museum, Hendon. Captures the   **David Askham**
essence of the museum far better than a simple shot of the building itself.

Similar arguments apply to the cost factor. Is it worthwhile commissioning a photographer to spend days or weeks on a job, possibly in a foreign land, when it would clearly be cheaper to find a stock solution? The decision would rest on how important the client regards hiring a highly-specialised big name photographer and the size of the financial budget.

Bearing in mind the above considerations, in this chapter we will look at the following major market sectors traditionally served by photo libraries: book publishing, consumer magazine editorial, advertising, public relations, and calendars and greetings cards.

Inevitably there is some overlap between these arbitrary divisions. For example, some consumer magazines publish "advertorials" – a hybrid feature written essentially for an advertiser. These resemble impartial editorial articles, but in small print you may find the phrase: "Special Promotion". Such ploys bolster advertising sales, but inevitably some readers can be confused as they fail to recognise advertising in disguise.

A similar overlap occurs with calendars, which are not only published by specialist publishers, but by provincial newspapers, magazines, and advertising agencies – the latter on behalf of their clients.

So we come to the aim of this chapter, which is to appraise the primary markets traditionally served by photo libraries. This should assist

Filming taking place in Polperro harbour, Cornwall. Adds interest to an otherwise standard view of a popular tourist spot. **David Askham**

both contributing photographers and new libraries to orientate their work towards meeting the strict requirements of at least some of these markets.

Book publishing

A prodigious number of books are published every year and – despite the fact that a significant number are ultimately remaindered at cut-prices or eventually pulped – this huge market appears to have an almost insatiable appetite for photographic illustrations.

Of course we are looking here mainly at the non-fiction sector of publishing, which is by far the bigger category. However fictional books sometimes use photography, even if only as part of a graphic design, on their dust covers.

Photographs used in book publishing are often provided by directly commissioned specialist photographers. Sometimes photographs are supplied by the authors themselves. But a large proportion of book illustrations are obtained from photo libraries, as testified by scrutiny of the photography credits pages.

Because we live in a visual age, book publishers have learned that profusely illustrated books have wide appeal and generate satisfying sales. But the photographic illustrations have to be absolutely relevant to the theme and text of a book, and also have to be of a suitably high quality. Failure to meet either of these criteria is likely to have a seriously adverse affect on the success of the book once published.

Recognition of this fact by photo libraries is very important. It is a total waste of everyone's time and money for a library to send out sub-standard photographs, or subjects which do not meet the picture researcher's precise requirements accurately.

Let us spend a moment looking in more detail at picture relevance.

Picture relevance

Good picture researchers will try to interpret a book publishing editor's requirements as carefully as possible, following meetings between all concerned.

The decision to use photographs of specific subjects is a value judgment. In each case, one of the questions asked should be: will a reader grasp the significance of the narrative or description better if a specific point is illustrated with a photograph? If so, then a detailed picture requirement can be added to the list.

At the end of the process a check will be made to ensure that a good balance has been reached between the textual and photographic content of the planned book.

This is only the start of the picture selection process. Much later, when the picture researcher has obtained a range of suitable pictures, the art director or designer will have a significant influence on which photographs are chosen and how they will fit in with the budget.

So far we have assumed that photographs are required only to complement commissioned text. Occasionally it works the other way round – the concept for a new book may be based predominantly on pictorial content.

Sometimes such a book will have been conceived to feature the work of one or more celebrated photographers. Obviously there is little requirement in that case for photo library stock unless the photographer was an early pioneer and their work has been dispersed. But often a publisher will choose a popular theme, such as dogs or cats or gardens, and seek the entire range of photographs from stock photo libraries.

Book publishing waxes and wanes according to the economic cycles. Some years photo libraries cannot find enough relevant pictures to meet the demand. In other years, when book publishing is in the doldrums, they have to look to other markets.

Periodical publishing

Consumer magazines represent one of the biggest markets supplied by photo libraries and it would be a rare library that has not supplied this market at some time. Some, in fact, specialise in it entirely.

The reason for this popularity is the great diversity of subjects covered in the periodical press. Thousands of titles are published and many have an almost insatiable appetite for photographs. For example, there is rarely any aspect of human behaviour, both past and present, or the natural and scientific worlds, which fails to generate a need for pictures, many of which can be supplied from stock photo libraries.

It was once the custom for magazines to retain photographers on their staff, especially if the nature of the subjects called for specialist knowledge and topical coverage. As financial pressures increased over the years, the numbers of permanent photographic staff employed by magazine publishers were drastically reduced. Many photographers were made redundant, their place taken by commercial and freelance photographers commissioned to cover specific editorial photographic requirements.

Wisley Gardens, Surrey. Foregrounding the pool and garden   **David Askham**
emphasises the nature of this famous horticultural centre.

But not all picture requirements can be met in this way. Often the only route to finding suitable pictures is through a photo library, particularly when the subjects sought are not quickly and easily accessible.

An additional factor is cost. In many cases it may also prove more economical to use stock pictures from a library.

Calendars and greetings cards

Photo libraries supply a lot of photographic material to publishers of calendars and greetings cards, a category which can also include other associated stationery products such as product packaging, bookmarks

Idyllic beach scenes with palm trees and blue sky have endless appeal to picture buyers.

David Askham

and wrapping paper.

The calendar and greetings cards markets are very specialised. It should also be recognised that many calendar and greetings cards publishers use a lot of non-photographic artwork, such as modern original drawings and paintings, old copyright-free pictures and even pure graphic art.

This diversity serves to underline the fact that photography does not have a clear run in this market sector, as a check of any display of greetings cards will testify.

Some calendar and greetings card subjects are very susceptible to changes in fashion. Others have to meet extremely stringent client requirements. Often these tightly directed artistic requirements can only be met by famous named photographers who are specially commissioned.

Certain art buyers have clear preferences for specific styles and will accept none other. But in contrast, many more publishers have more broadly-based requirements which can be amply met by stock photo libraries. The libraries understand this particular market very well and enjoy considerable and continuing success supplying it.

Many pictures suitable for these markets, such as scenic landscapes, can have a timeless quality which confers on them long and useful lives. So photo libraries like to recruit contributing photographers who can regularly keep them supplied with this type of timeless picture, especially those strong in conveying atmospheric moods. At the same time though, for other markets, they may want the same photographers to supply up-to-date views of urban or tourist subjects, which can change with remarkable speed as new building developments take place.

Apart from scenic subjects, animals and flowers are the two other highly popular subjects for use on both calendars and greetings cards. Just imagine the potential multitude of opportunities for photographers working to meet this demand.

However, even with such universally popular subjects, publishers have to take account of widely variable customer preferences. For example, in the north of England, there was a time when consumers favoured greetings cards illustrated with specific types of flowers which, for some reason, were less popular in the south. With animals, there is a clear demand for photographs of young animals rather than mature specimens.

So there is no universal solution where pictorial subjects for this market are concerned. In addition, one has to take account of constantly fluctuating changes in fashion and likes and dislikes. Only the best-informed photo libraries with foresight as well as a good breadth and depth of stock are able to maintain sales to these particular publishers.

Advertising

The advertising industry is a big-budget sector. The industry's clients include some of the biggest international corporations, which have grown big at least partly as a result of the successful marketing of their products. It is in support of these marketing operations that advertising agencies make such an important contribution. Because available budgets are usually so large, it is understandable that competition among the agencies who are bidding for such work is fierce.

In this area, where picture buyers usually have a sizable budget to work with, it is easy to see why fees available for the use of stock photographs are some of the most generous available. But there are other good reasons. A chosen photograph may be reproduced as a major element of a vast billboard poster, possibly published nationwide or even worldwide. It would have to be a very good photograph, but there is a down-side – the subsequent wide exposure to public gaze might inhibit future use of the picture in other forms of media. That is one reason why pictures used in advertising campaigns earn significantly higher fees than when they are used, for example, on straightforward editorial pages.

Of course, advertising is not only about producing big posters; it covers the promotion of a client's products in most sectors of the media. It can include television and cinema commercials, advertisements in consumer and trade magazines, and the publication of company annual reports, sales catalogues, brochures and allied publications. There is scarcely a sphere of modern life untouched by the power of advertising. So it is unsurprising that photo libraries are keen to secure a share of those sizable financial budgets.

As to the type of picture used, let us take a small example. A leading national building society wanted to promote its new Individual Savings Account – or ISA – ahead of the national launch of that method of saving. It chose the phrase "A Perfect Environment to Grow your Tax-free Savings" and used a photograph of a small domestic greenhouse to complement the words. The chosen picture, inspired by the copywriter's use of the key word "grow", is typical of the way a fairly ordinary photograph can be used in advertising.

There is a further reason why advertising continues to be an important market for photo libraries. During the research for this book, several respondents highlighted the fact that fees for photographs used in advertising were practically alone in keeping pace with inflation over the past ten years. That is an interesting reflection on relative values and financial reward.

Public relations

Public relations is sometimes assumed to be part of the service advertising agencies perform for their clients. Occasionally that is true, but more usually it is provided by independent specialist public relations agencies, or in-house specialist departments of larger businesses or organisations. They serve their clients by organising publicity events, issuing press releases on newsworthy subjects, and acting as a catalyst in procuring media exposure.

Where clients produce tangible products, any photographic needs are easily met by special commissions. But many clients are in business to offer a service to their particular markets, and it is less easy to depict the nature or special characteristics of a service.

It is to meet such nebulous requirements that public relations agencies call on photo libraries for pictorial solutions. In many ways, such picture requirements for public relations are similar to those given in the example above for advertising agencies.

PICTURE REQUIREMENTS

On the face of it, selecting photographs from a stock photo library to meet the subjects listed on a client's "wants list" is a fairly straightforward process. While in many cases this assumption may be true, many picture researchers will tell you stories to the contrary.

So let us look at how meeting picture requirements works in the real world.

Matching needs

Problems arise in two areas. The first arises from a photo library's lack of matching stock. Inevitably there are gaps in the picture files, either as a result of available stock already having been sent out to other clients, or simply because the library does not hold pictures which meet the picture researcher's requirements exactly.

The second problem arises from the wording used to describe specific pictures on the list. Transcription errors can also lead to many a wild goose chase. Vague requirements, such as "I want a white cat", or "Anything on Wales" (when they possibly mean whales!), may only result in wasted search time, unnecessary costs and a disappointed client. Often a few details of how the picture is intended to be used would help the library researcher and avoid dissatisfaction.

A lot of the above problems can be avoided by picture researchers limiting their search to well-organised specialist photo libraries. Specialist libraries are more likely to have a good depth of subject matter in stock as well as a matching specialist knowledge of those subjects. The latter is quite important in helping researchers find exactly what they need, and can sometimes tip the scales in the selection process.

However, despite this seeming advantage, BAPLA reports that there is a trend among some picture researchers to favour "one stop shopping" in the hope that one library can satisfy all their needs.

Highest quality

Now for a few words on picture quality. In order to be competitive, publishers naturally strive to deliver a top quality product, though obviously within agreed budgetary constraints. Superlative photography is an implicit part of this requirement. Therefore it is understandable that decision-makers will not accept any material which does not meet their high standards.

That is why photo libraries have learned to acquire and supply only the best quality images. In turn, that means that only correctly exposed and critically sharp colour transparencies, with fully saturated colours, will be acceptable. If one particular photo library cannot supply such pictures, other competing ones almost certainly will. That is why contributing photographers are obliged consistently to meet the highest quality standards.

Many photo libraries advise their contributing photographers to use only specified film stock for their photography. For example, Fuji Velvia is renowned for its rich colour saturation, sharpness and slightly larger-than-life colours, which seem to appeal to many publishers. That advice has been generated from the hard experience of what the markets demand.

Libraries sometimes even go further and urge that films should be processed only by laboratories catering for professional photographers. Such commonsense advice should be heeded and not viewed as intrusive interference.

Good presentation is another aspect which distinguishes the best photo libraries from the rest. The use of standardised mounts is an obvious factor, but so is the use of clear labelling and library identification.

As far as captions are concerned there is no doubt that comprehensive picture information, though edited for conciseness, will always find

An evocative seasonal vision of spring, incorporating elements that would appeal across a range of potential markets.   **David Askham**

favour with clients. Where seasonality or timing is relevant, such as the precise month when a specific flower was photographed, it is important to include this information on the label. The same holds true for locations of scenic photographs.

Traditional subjects

What do we mean by traditional subjects? My interpretation is that traditional subjects are those which have historically been made widely available by stock photo libraries. These are the run-of-the-mill subjects which are constantly in demand. They include people, places, buildings, the trappings of modern life, and human activities in the widest sense.

Holiday places and business destinations are constantly in demand, and many major libraries initially made their names in supplying the insatiable market for such pictures. Success for the pioneers spawned increasing competition as new libraries were set up to cash in on this lucrative range of subjects.

Although the market may now be saturated, there is likely to be no decline in the demand for excellent and up-to-date pictures of world-wide destinations. Apart from the wide spectrum of holiday images, with the growth in leisure time and a continually expanding generation in retirement from full-time work there is a growing requirement for pictures illustrating leisure activities such as gardening, do-it-yourself projects and sports.

Finally, there is also a growing demand for model-released pictures of human interest and family activities, so-called lifestyle images. Although producing acceptable photographs in this field is quite challenging, this could remain one of the main growth areas in the foreseeable future.

Beyond the norm

It is difficult to gauge the market for truly innovative photographs. Their appeal is mainly to those buyers who are seeking examples of interpretive and artistic photography of the kind that can be found in specialist galleries, though expressionist photography is sometimes commissioned by advertising agencies to meet exploratory concepts.

However, some libraries maintain special sections for avant-garde or abstract subjects, knowing that they have clients who occasionally seek unusual images to form part of a graphic art design.

The growth of interest in computer generated or modified digital images has been apparent for some time. It has spawned a limited degree of specialisation among some photographers who possess the artistic ability to produce such pictures to a high standard. But by the very nature of the images it is extremely difficult to anticipate customer demands, and that hurdle probably accounts for the limited demand and well as supply of finished digital images. Often a publisher's concept may only be met by specially commissioned work.

However, digital photography is expanding rapidly and the time may well come when stock images produced and generated digitally become widely accepted and marketed. This section of the market is, of course, distinct from digitised distribution of conventionally produced stock photography.

THE DECISION-MAKERS

In the business world, most managers have a general or specific responsibility to make decisions which can have an impact on the conduct of their company's business. However, for the purpose of this book, the focus will be on those individuals who have the most direct influence on which of many pictures supplied by competing photo libraries will be selected for publication.

This relatively narrow and specialised field of decision-makers ranges from editors of prestigious glossy magazines or coffee table books, to small public relations account holders who only occasionally draw on photo libraries for stock photographs.

Beyond this group lies another important layer of people who directly, or indirectly, influence those whose primary responsibility is picture selection. In a word, they are likely to be accountants (the "suits" as one manager termed them). They set and monitor budgets for specific projects and thus set the financial boundaries within which editors and picture researchers operate.

But apart from noting their existence, we will consider only those people who have a direct influence on the business done with photo libraries.

Editors

The term editor covers a very wide range of decision-makers. Job descriptions vary from one business to another. As a generalisation, however, most editors have a responsibility for bringing together both words and artwork to meet their publishers' policy directives.

I think it would also be true to say that most editors are, primarily, writers or journalists. Words are, therefore, their natural stock in trade. So, unless they have picture specialists on their staff, when it comes to selecting photographs to integrate with text or other artwork, their criteria for selection will vary considerably and will generally be very subjective.

Some general editors will be very discriminating when choosing photographs and will know precisely what they want. Others will be less discerning and accept almost anything that helps to fill a page. Editors are human beings, who are frequently under a lot of stress, which is why it is so important to develop good working relationships with them.

In bigger publishing organisations editors are assisted by picture editors or art editors who undertake the important role of assembling the relevant pictures needed for publication. In this situation the editor or editor-in-chief may or may not have a final say in which images are chosen. However the editor does have ultimate responsibility for the content and appearance of their publication, and is unlikely to abrogate that important role.

Art directors, art editors or picture editors, (the title is not necessarily interchangeable), generally have a background of training and experience in some field of art or design. Their roles often include graphic design, which is a crucial element in publishing because the success of a publication can be favourably or unfavourably influenced by the overall quality of its design.

As a part of their duties, these specialised editors have a pivotal role in commissioning new photography or using pictures from a photo library. They may be assisted by other staff or freelance picture researchers, but the ultimate decision is theirs. Quite often, too, it is the art editor who manages the budget for photography.

Picture researchers

We now come to the most important group of decision-makers – picture researchers. They are important because they are usually the people who have the most direct contact with photo libraries.

On a personal level, picture researchers represent the human faces and voices of a photo library's clients. It is they who make the first selection of pictures, often, though not invariably, following a visit to the libraries. It is normal practise for them to send out lists of pictures required, which are used by the photo libraries' own picture researching staff to assemble appropriate packages of suitable pictures.

Picture researchers often have an artistic background, but not always. Certainly they need to be able to interpret a publisher's needs as far as pictures are concerned.

They also require the investigative skills of a detective, an agile mind, and the intelligence to get to the heart of often obscure and specialised subject matter.

Advertising and PR

As discussed earlier in this chapter, a considerable number of stock photographs are used by advertising and public relations agencies. So who selects these pictures?

The simple answer is almost anyone connected with the relevant account. In a small agency, key staff tend to cover many facets of the agency's creative work, while in a bigger concern, an account holder will either directly, or indirectly, decide what artwork is to be used.

Because there is no standardised organisation, photo libraries have to learn who is responsible and take time to brief the client on the library's specific strengths.

Often, as relationships are built up, a photo library may suggest new stock subjects to its contributors in order to build up a suitable pool of appropriate photography.

Other markets

Many clients of photo libraries fall outside the categories outlined above. Graphic designers sometimes have the responsibility for selecting pictures for use in a wide range of applications. Makers of jigsaw puzzles, calendars, packaging, labels and a myriad of specialist products can fall into this category.

What is important is that photo libraries identify the key decision-makers and make sure they are kept appraised of what new material is added to their stock.

Some successful photo libraries carve quite a niche for themselves in finding less well known and often obscure markets for their stock pictures. Newly established photo libraries could do worse than target the less well publicised sectors.

Market fluidity

In the world of business, it is safe to assume that supply and demand, and trading conditions, will always be in a state of flux. Commercial activity is always affected by recurring economic cycles.

If the world suffers from an economic recession, it is highly unlikely that photo libraries will be immune from the financial consequences. The converse is equally true: when the world economy is booming and the diverse cross-section of picture libraries' clients are enjoying growth, then it is reasonable to assume that well-stocked, competent and well-administered libraries will share in that success.

As with any business, however, photo libraries operate in a highly competitive world and only the best will survive.

Another distinguishing feature of modern commercial life is the fact that there is no longer such a condition as a career for life. People in business seem to be constantly on the move, for a variety of reasons. Sometimes it is in the interests of career progression, possibly for further education, or merely key personnel seeking new pastures. Occasionally it is the result of company mergers, takeovers or plain reorganisation.

In addition, many major publishing houses have changed ownership during recent years; inevitably philosophies and company policies suffer changes.

Whatever the cause, the negative effect of such turbulence is that working relationships between photo library staff, their clients and their contributing photographers are disrupted – randomly and regularly.

Some examples will illustrate how this fluidity affects the business and requirements of a photo library.

Ranges of books may be discontinued or changed significantly, thus impacting adversely on the demand for, and hence the supply of, new photographs. Photo libraries may already have set in train the procurement of new images in anticipation of client requirements, and it is doubtful that compensation clauses could be invoked to underwrite the costs incurred by an unexpected change.

A second example concerns the photo library to external picture researcher relationship, which is probably the most fruitful conduit for business. It takes time to build up a good working relationship, which is invariably strengthened by past successes.

When a publisher's in-house picture researcher is replaced, possibly by a freelance, there is no guarantee that the replacement will continue to patronise specific photo libraries in the same way as the predecessor. Suddenly, business with an established client is ended or disrupted.

Conversely, of course, other photo libraries may then benefit from new business.

MAINTAINING AN EDGE

Having observed that there is, generally speaking, an over-supply of many photographic subjects in stock photo libraries, consideration must be given to ways of winning and maintaining a competitive edge in the marketplace.

Timing is a vital element in meeting market requirements. It is probably true to say that any photographic subject, no matter when it was conceived, has the potential for publication at some time or other – but this potential will fluctuate through time. The timeliness of responding to a client's request is another aspect of how the time factor can influence the photo library business.

We will look at these two aspects in more detail below.

Different approaches

Photographers should take heart from the fact that there are an infinite number of ways of photographing many subjects. They should be constantly seeking alternative styles, angles, and treatments of the subjects they choose to tackle. By all means start with the classic views, but be on the look-out for a means of portraying your subjects in a very personal way.

This is a test of photographic abilities and a challenge to master new techniques. Often a view can be improved by imaginative framing, subtle composition, disguised use of colour filters, inclusion of foreground interest, or sensitive use of human interest.

Landscape photographers are blessed with infinite patience and will wait for days, weeks, or even longer to capture unique lighting effects which mark out their work as that of top professionals. Thus it is often the taking of inestimable care which enables a photographer to gain that elusive competitive edge.

It may sound daunting, but if you wonder why your excellent work is failing to gain the recognition you anticipated, look beyond the obvious approaches and identify how you can add something unique to the quality and value of your photography.

Aging images

Theoretically all stock library photographs have the potential to find a market. In practice, only a minority do. Most languish in library files until they are filtered out and returned to their contributors, a kind of annual spring cleaning practised by the more efficient photo libraries.

If you were able to plot sales against time elapsed since a photograph was taken, it would surely show that the newest and freshest photographs have the greater sales potential, essentially because they reflect the contemporary scene. Editors are constantly searching for images which illustrate the world today and the current activities of its peoples.

When the pendulum of time swings to the other extreme, you will find stock pictures which are retained by photo libraries for their historical interest. Those pictures still have sales potential, but probably not on the same scale as contemporary pictures unless belonging to an era whose nostalgia becomes a temporary vogue.

It is surprising how quickly many photographs become dated. Changes in fashion, particularly in human dress and hair styles, is an obvious example. The pace of technological change also contributes to unavoidable dating of photographic images. The style of transportation even a decade ago would characterise an image as dated. Consider, also, the growth of urban development and the way city skylines have changed. Earthquakes and similar natural disasters also change the face of our planet.

Taken together, you can see why photo libraries which specialise in travel, for example, have to ensure that their stock is updated almost on an annual basis.

Nevertheless, some subject areas, such as the natural world and abstracts, are largely untouched by the time element.

Finally, of course, photographs themselves degrade over time, as colour saturation diminishes or particular dyes fade. This is more marked with certain film types and can be influenced by variable processing standards.

Business time-scales

Another aspect of time concerns business practice and the time-scales for average transactions.

Many new contributing photographers initially fail to appreciate the relatively long periods of time which elapse between the despatch of pictures from a library until they are returned by the client. Then there is a further accounting delay of several weeks, or possibly many months, particularly when a book project is involved and payment is not made until the month after the date of publication.

However, even that is not the end of the story. Fees have to be split between several photographers as part of the internal accounting within the libraries. So most libraries aggregate picture sales on a quarterly basis and send out cheques to their contributing photographers four times a year. It is not uncommon for the overall period covering each picture sale to be up to one year, sometimes even longer. That is why new contributors often have to wait a year or more before seeing any return at all from photographs accepted by their chosen photo library.

The above consideration assumes that pictures will actually sell. However, it should also be realised that a high proportion of stock pictures lies dormant in libraries for many years awaiting an opportunity to be selected to meet a requirement. Many pictures are never chosen and eventually are returned to the photographer unsold. That is a potentially discouraging, but inevitable, fact of photo library life.

Profile

Skyscan Photolibrary

The Skyscan Photolibrary was launched in 1984, essentially to capitalise on a growing volume of specialist aerial photography produced by Andy Marks. While commercial photography continues to make a successful contribution to the business, it is the library, which is run by Andy's wife Brenda and their assistant Phill, which has really taken off in recent times.

Andy Marks spent his early working life in engineering until takeovers and redundancy gave him the opportunity to launch his own business. Initially he developed a commercial enterprise flying advertising balloons, with two secondary services, one of which was aerial photography from his tethered balloon. He developed and perfected a system which allowed him to recover the helium gas after use and to use television monitoring to align his cameras accurately. Soon the latter became the most successful strand of his new business and he quickly found a worthwhile niche market for his aerial photography.

In his early days aerial photography was done to meet his clients' requirements, but Andy soon saw the opportunity, whilst out and about, to take other images for Skyscan's own portfolio. Two books based on their photographs added to their collection and became the basis for the unique and highly specialised library.

Although Skyscan's aerial photography continues to serve the needs of an impressive list of corporate clients, it is the photo library side of the business which has grown more quickly. Whereas at launch, commissioned photography contributed around 70% of income, the ratio is now roughly reversed with the photo library being the major contributor. Library clients are mainly in the editorial, advertising, calendar and book publishing sectors.

Part of the reason for the continuing success of the library was the decision to seek and represent a carefully selected number of specialist

Promotional montage image incorporating many of the elements of Skyscan's subject range.

The Skyscan Photolibrary

contributing photographers whose work would complement Skyscan's, without duplicating or competing with images already on file. Currently there are about sixty professional or talented semi-pro photographers who cover, for example, aerial sports, hot air ballooning and air-to-air photography. The library now comprises over 90,000 Skyscan images

75

and about 25,000 pictures from contributing photographers.

But the enterprise did not stop there. An interesting marketing initiative saw the launch of The Specialist Source, which is a loose federation of around 20–30 unique, small photo libraries. The advantage for clients is that they can approach any photo library in the group, which then becomes the "Contact Library". The picture requests are then filtered and passed to the appropriate libraries who can respond directly to the client. All negotiations are conducted through the initial contact library.

Such an arrangement is popular with researchers because it saves them time and possibly multiple search fees. It is also very useful to specialist libraries because they are connected to potential clients they may never have found themselves.

Brenda Marks explained: "Between us, we can offer a service equivalent to a large general library. We are the aerial specialists. Other libraries in the group cover, for example, mountaineering, ecology, applied science, crafts, defence, yacht racing, astronomy, alternative medicine, golf and many more niche areas.

"It doesn't work for all libraries. Some are far too narrowly specialised. Although we are nominally an aerial photography library, our subject range is vast and covers every imaginable type of building and landscape features. For example, we recently received a request for a picture to illustrate the Holy Trinity, an abstract subject open to interpretation. We satisfied the client with a picture of a very unusual building whose architect designed into it three of everything; three sides, three chimneys and so on. That example shows the value of knowing your picture stock intimately and being able to think laterally. The client was very pleased with the solution."

An increasingly important element of the Skyscan library's work is the capability to source aerial images from unique, largely unknown, collections of historic aerial photography which are not part of the Skyscan library. For example, lawyers retained to resolve boundary disputes appreciate the research Skyscan can perform and are very willing to pay a fee for their research services and reports.

Investing in new technology is a daunting decision for most small photo libraries. Is it wise to spend up to £1,000 purely for a third party to design, set up and run an Internet website for a small library, particularly when the rewards are difficult to quantify?

Any doubters should talk to Brenda Marks, whose infectious enthusiasm helps solve such dilemmas. Her first generation website cost a mere £80! How did she do it?

"I enrolled at a local night school. A ten-week course (one evening a week) cost me £60 and a book on web design another £20. At the end of the course I had our website up and running."

She confessed that she can see that it can now be improved, but she has gained valuable experience, for little investment, and knows that a "phase two" investment of time and modest funds can be justified.

Having seen how Brenda, largely self-taught, has introduced computing into the business, such confidence and enthusiasm can only lead to further success. What advice would she give to a talented photographer who seriously wishes to become a contributing photographer to an established photo library?

"Unless they have some really stunning pictures which might be accepted and succeed with a large library, they would be better placing their work with an active, well-renowned specialist library."

And is working in a picture library fun?

"Yes. It is challenging, different, visually stunning, creative, with no two days the same. It is invigorating being in the forefront of some of the most exciting and fastest moving changes in the electronic medium. I find it enormously stimulating. I only wish I had more time to indulge in learning, perfecting and experimenting."

It is difficult to forget Skyscan's infectious enthusiasm for their work.

4.   Selecting
         a Library

Welcome to new readers who have skipped the earlier chapters in their restless quest for a quick answer to the question: How do I choose the best photo library for me?

If there was an easy answer to this question you probably would not have bought this book in the first place. But life is not that simple. Hence this important chapter which will address the subject in some detail so that, by the end, readers should have discovered a effective route through the decision-making process. But first, consider some anecdotes typical of many ambitious photographers.

I am frequently approached by aspiring contributing photographers for advice. I ask them what material they have to offer a library. A typical response is: "Oh, I have just come back from Africa (or America, or some remote wilderness) and I have some fantastic pictures. How can I recoup some of my costs?"

I ask them what else they have to offer. The usual answer is – very little.

A recent telephone inquirer was an expert photographer of stags in the wild. Nothing else, just stags beautifully illuminated in their natural environment. He told me that his life-long ambition has been to shoot the perfect image of this subject and friends had suggested that he should get an agency to represent his specialist collection.

I knew that he was a very talented photographer. In fact a leading national newspaper and a country magazine had published some of his pictures and there was no doubt about his competence. So he sent some of his best photographs to a photo library specialising in natural history. But, after consideration, they had declined to recruit him because they "...already had his subject well covered".

So I asked him what else he had to offer? Nothing! When I suggested that he should broaden his approach to the subject, possibly covering

*An example of a typical subject selection as contained in photo
library catalogues and promotional literature.*

the life cycle of deer as a first step, he was repulsed by the idea. I sensed
that my course of action would deflect him from his extremely narrow,
but none-the-less worthy pursuit.

While I have the greatest respect for this photographer, he provides a good example of why many highly competent photographers fail to become contributors to commercial photo libraries. When their love is pure photography and they shy away from the less appealing prospects of diversification and administration, it is clear that their photographic goals are incompatible with the needs of providing consistent support to a library.

Those two examples may appear to offer a somewhat negative approach to the subject of choosing a photo library. However they do illustrate the need to filter out those photographers who, for various reasons, are probably temperamentally unsuited to the commercial realities of becoming serious contributors.

THE ANALYTICAL APPROACH

So what is the best way to tackle this difficult task of choosing a good and appropriate photo library? My approach is unashamedly analytical, because I have witnessed too many disappointed flirtations by impulsive photographers who believe the road to riches is a simple one. This chapter will address:

- Identifying your subject coverage and areas of expertise;
- Listing the criteria for selecting a photo library;
- Researching potential libraries;
- Studying photo libraries' information packs;
- Prioritising potential libraries;
- Selecting and submitting sample photographs;
- Organising a one-to-one interview;
- Final decision.

Self analysis

The first task is to identify what you have already achieved, photographically. Ask yourself: if you were compelled to start marketing your stock of photographs today, what would you have to offer?

That question sounds simple enough, but could you easily supply the answer?

Possibly not, because not all photographers systematically categorise, caption and file their best photographs. It is human nature to turn to the next project soon after receiving, reviewing and disposing of the latest results.

However, for those well disciplined individuals who store their photographic stock in an orderly fashion, it should be a fairly straightforward exercise to examine subject categories and assess their strengths, standards and potential as stock library pictures. Rubbish and the inevitable sub-standard photographs, such as exposure bracketed variants, should long ago have been pruned out of the collection.

Regardless of the storage and recording methods you use, it is essential to take a retrospective and objective look at the photography you have produced over the past few years. List the subject areas in which you have extensive high-quality stock. Re-order this list so that the most important and impressive categories are at the top. In an adjacent column quantify each category.

If you work in more than one film format, split the quantity column to show how much stock you have in each film size (some photo libraries limit the ranges of film formats they market).

If your records are sufficiently complete, add another column to the above chart to show the approximate annual production rate for each category. This information is very useful if a prospective librarian asks you how many new images you are likely to be able to contribute per annum. Even if they do not probe this aspect, the information is a good pointer to your own future planning and budgeting.

Your chart might look a little like the following after five years photography:

Subject	Quantities		Annual Production		
	6x7cm	35mm	6x7cm	35mm	All formats
Architecture	5,500	750	1,100	150	1,250
British landscape	1,000	500	200	'100	300
Meteorology	100	1,000	20	200	220
Water-sports	0	500	0	100	100

It is clear from these fictitious figures that architecture is the main strength of this particular photographer, although hidden among the minority subjects may well be material sufficiently unusual to merit promotion. For example, water-sports may be a relatively new area of interest taken up only in the last year. If it is thought likely to be sustained in the future, the subject might well merit second place in the league table.

Younger readers, possibly fresh from art or photographic training,

may well feel like giving up at this point. They may not have been prac-
tising serious photography long enough to have built up sufficient qual-
ifying stock.

Bear in mind that photo libraries will typically (though not always)
want to see a minimum of one hundred colour transparencies as a first
submission. You will need many more than that number to give yourself
some choice in compiling your initial test contribution.

Consider a non-photographic example; one in the horticultural
world. Growers of specimen flowers think nothing of growing and trans-
porting a van-load of potential prize-winning roses, chrysanthemums or
sweet peas to a major flower show and then spending hours selecting
merely a dozen or so of the very best to exhibit. Nothing is left to
chance, and making a selection for your first submission to a library is
not very different.

However figures alone do not tell the whole story; they are merely a
useful tool for analysis. But self-analysis does not stop there. Other factors may need to be taken into account.

Personal factors

Some other factors are quite difficult to quantify. For example, how do
you represent your performance patterns, consistency of photographic
quality, personal preferences as far as subjects are concerned, tenacity
when confronted by set-backs, or measure perseverance in the face of
adversity?

Ignore these factors if you wish, but if we are to be honest they can
have a considerable bearing on our ability to maintain a consistent supply of saleable photographs to a photo library. Life is seldom one long
smooth sailing. There are high points and low points, and recognition of
these factors does help us to temper our ambitions and plan more realistic projections or forecasts of potential achievement.

Assuming that you have some prior experience in marketing your
work, how imaginative are you in interpreting market requirements?
Many photographers make the mistake of trying to emulate images
already in print and which are readily available from many photo
libraries. They are merely adding to the vast pool of similar material and
reducing their chances of succeeding.

Successful contributors look beyond the obvious and try to deliver
new photographs which have a fresh and distinctive appearance about
them. They are prepared to develop an individualistic style which distinguishes their work from the majority. It is not easy, but possible, and

Photofusion

17a Electric Lane
London SW9 8LA
Tel: 0171-738-5774
Fax: 0171-738-5509
www: photofusion.org
E-mail: library@photofusion.org

*Agencies do not only deal in the straightforward stock image. Some
specialise in material of a more social documentary nature.*

should always be one of your aims.

Before leaving market research, it is useful to consider how capable you are of anticipating future market trends and requirements. The ability to anticipate new requirements may seem little more than crystal ball gazing. But maintaining a constant awareness of what is happening in the world, through regular study of the media and perceptive observation of life around you, often provides the impetus to pursue new projects in anticipation of demand. It can provide an edge that others lack.

Financial factors

Leading on from this last point, are you willing to travel, if necessary, to places that are not particularly appealing to you, regardless of weather or personal circumstances? And could you afford the financial outlay even if the potential benefits exceeded the projected costs?

If the answers to these questions are "no", you might be courting failure if thinking of make travel photography your main core activity, because offerings limited to those culled from your annual holiday may not be sufficient to generate the desired level of sales. Remember, also, that many travel pictures quickly become dated and need replacing.

You cannot escape from the need for budgetary control. Do you know precisely how much you spend each year on new equipment, repairs, insurance, consumables and other expenses in shooting stock photography? If you do know, could you increase that budget if necessary; for example, to generate increased revenue to meet growing demands from those who need your support?

Is your photographic equipment sufficiently rugged, reliable, relevant and of a professional standard for producing quality stock photography regularly for the foreseeable future? If not, have you funds for remedying the situation?

How good are your administrative, record-keeping and accounting capabilities? Do you suffer from ill-health or from any incapacities which could limit your working regime? Again, these are important questions which have a bearing on your ability to run a small business activity, in this case one of supplying one or more photo libraries with regular new stock.

This section has been an exercise in self-examination, discovering more about our strengths and weaknesses. If you skip over these considerations, your chances of building a successful relationship with a photo library may be seriously diminished.

Or, like our ambitious deer-hunting photographer, you may wish to avoid disappointment by recognising that the role of a contributing photographer is not for you. In that case the price of this book may already have saved you potentially wasted future investment.

84

SELECTING A LIBRARY

If you decide to buy a new car, you are unlikely to wander into a dealer's showroom without having previously decided, more-or-less, what features you are seeking. You will know roughly what size of car and engine you need; how many doors it should have; and whether it should be a saloon, hatchback or estate car.

You wouldn't necessarily recognise these as selection criteria, but they are and you would instinctively measure possible new cars against your list of essential and desirable characteristics – all within a budget, of course.

This example of identifying selection criteria is equally valid when selecting a photo library. So what criteria should we consider?

Subjects

Fairly obviously, the first step is to identify the main picture subjects which you plan to offer a library. This is crucial because it will help narrow the field of potential libraries. But if the subjects are quite different, such as those tabulated earlier in this chapter, it may be necessary to target one or more specialist photo libraries.

Some subjects range very widely in scope. For example, consider travel again. Some of the bigger general libraries attempt to cover every geographical possibility. They are part of a global network with contributing photographers based in many different countries. Other libraries specialise in discrete areas or countries, such as Bryan and Cherry Alexander who mainly cover the polar and neighbouring regions.

So if your specialisation is travel, it is important to itemise the continents, countries, counties or regions for which you already have good in-depth coverage and are likely to continue to photograph in the future.

How many top quality pictures are you able to offer in the first instance? Most libraries require to see a specific number of sample images, so you need to be able to match their requirements.

Also identify the maximum number of pictures per annum that you can realistically hope to supply to a photo library. Again, some photo libraries may wish to be reassured of the strength of your future commitment.

A further criterion concerns film formats. If you produce photography in a range of formats and you expect to continue your operations with each of those formats, there is no point being attracted to a photo library that will not accept the full range of your output. That is unless

If you are a genuine specialist in any subject, it makes sense to begin by approaching the specialist libraries in that field.

WINDRUSH PHOTOS
THE BIRD SPECIALISTS

unless you are prepared to change your approach or target more than one photo library.

However, do recognise that libraries face great competition and, all other factors being equal, the larger film formats are generally more saleable for subjects where the formats are viable. There are obvious exceptions, such as active sports and wildlife photography, where 35mm equipment is clearly more appropriate and therefore acceptable.

Contracts

How long are you prepared to deposit your work with a specific library? It is not unusual to find that you could be contractually bound for up to five years.

Would you have any difficulty if there were exclusivity clauses which would limit your own marketing elsewhere? Some full-time globe-trotting travel photographers can only sustain the high costs of their operations by marketing their material with different libraries, possibly one or more in several different countries.

The question of exclusivity needs to be addressed quite seriously and contracts negotiated with care.

What is the maximum commission retained by a photo library which you would find acceptable?

For many years the normal rate has been 50% retained by the photo library and 50% paid to the contributing photographer. However, with allegedly higher costs of global marketing – a questionable point now that the Internet has, theoretically, shrunk the world – at least one major photo library is squeezing the terms imposed on their photographers. So it is important to decide your own minimum figure for commission.

An allied subject is the frequency of payments made to contributing photographers. Many libraries pay on a quarterly basis which most photographers find acceptable. A few libraries can be rather erratic in remitting fees to photographers, despite the widespread use of computerised accounting. Establish where you stand on this point.

Track records

Finally, you need to ascertain certain facts about the pedigree of a photo library. For example:

When was it established?
How diverse are its markets?
How many contributing photographers does it have on its books?
What are photographers' average earnings over three or more years?

Let us consider these criteria in turn.

If a photo library is very new, you would be taking a great deal on trust, because there would be no track record to examine. In contrast, if a library is decades old, there is a risk that the energy of the founders may have diminished unless new blood has been injected to meet the challenge of fast-changing markets and methods.

The diversity of the markets developed by a photo library is also revealing. Too extensive a range may stretch internal expertise, while too narrow a share of the available market sectors could set a clear ceiling on the library's earning potential.

Paradoxically, it could be argued that by specialising in serving the advertising sector for example, a library may have established recurring lucrative business by working closely with account holders and thereby generating regular commissions for the library and its contributing photographers.

Knowledge of the numbers of contributing photographers on a library's books can be useful in assessing the likely internal competition. Some photo libraries are meticulous in trying to avoid having too many photographers covering identical areas.

The final point, concerning average earnings, can be a very sensitive issue and you may find some libraries reluctant to discuss it. However, with tact it should be possible to obtain an approximation of average earnings, usually given as, for example, a small number of contributing photographers earning over £X,000 per annum with the rest averaging £Y. Any information on this topic can help in gauging your own targets as a contributing photographer.

Before leaving this section, make a list of the points which you consider relevant to helping you find a suitable photo library and make it part of your decision-making process.

RESEARCHING THE LIBRARIES

So far in this chapter we have been getting to know more about ourselves, our photographic ambitions and capabilities. Now it is time to consider how to produce a short-list of potential photo libraries which might match our talents and aspirations. So where do we begin?

A surprising number of photographers look at picture credits in newspapers and magazines in the hope of discovering who is supplying a variety of images. But credits only give a tiny fraction of the story. Many published pictures have no credits whatsoever, so the vast majority of published photographs will escape that analysis entirely. It is a very hit-and-miss approach to limit your research in this way.

Information sources

There are some useful sources of information on photo libraries published annually, or even more frequently.

Topical information is published in the Bureau of Freelance Photographers' monthly *Market Newsletter* in an "Agency News" section devoted to the current requirements of selected photo libraries.

The BFP also publishes the annual *Freelance Photographer's Market Handbook*, which amongst other listings has a section providing full details of over 100 libraries that are actively seeking work from new contributors. The listings contain details of ongoing requirements and terms of business, supported by a classified subject index. The book is an integral part of annual BFP membership, but can also be purchased separately.

Another useful reference book is the long-established *Writer's &*

Artist's Yearbook, which has a section on picture libraries and agencies. Note, however, that a number of the libraries listed therein do not take work from outside contributors.

For those interested in approaching libraries overseas, there are a number of sources to choose from.

For coverage of the picture library world internationally – though with the emphasis on Europe – several useful publications are obtainable from PIAG (Presse Informations Agentur GmbH) in Germany. These include the bi-monthly English language magazine for the picture trade, *Visuell International*, and the reference books *Picture Research, Photo Agencies and Libraries* and *Stock Photo Fees in Europe*. The latter two publications are produced in German/English and primarily designed for use by professional researchers and library staff, being a little expensive for the casual user. PIAG also has a comprehensive website.

For America there is the annual *Photographer's Market*, the US equivalent of the BFP's *Market Handbook*, containing details of over 200 stock photo agencies and their current picture requirements. It can be obtained in the UK direct from the BFP or from some specialist bookshops.

BAPLA can also supply, for a modest fee, two useful reference books covering international libraries – the CEPIC (Coordination of European Picture Agencies) directory covering Europe, and the PACA (Picture Agency Council of America) directory for the USA.

Contact details for all of the above will be found in the Useful Addresses section at the back of this book.

The Internet

For those readers with access to the Internet, the world is your oyster! First of all, try visiting BAPLA's website.

The BAPLA home page gives you a choice of learning more about the association (but see Annex I in this book for more information on BAPLA), or of referring to an index to BAPLA's membership with links to individual pages dedicated to each member library.

Each page contains essential contact information and a brief description of the library's subjects. In some cases you can link directly to the specific photo library's own website, but not all seem to have one at the time of writing. No doubt this situation will change as the benefits become clearer. If you do not have access to the Internet, search out public access in places like public libraries or "cyber-cafes".

It appears that most libraries which have invested in a Web site have done so primarily as an aid to marketing their stock, often including representative pictures for the benefit of picture researchers, but these can also be studied at leisure by photographers who are assessing a library from afar. However, a few libraries have provided a page or more of most useful information for prospective contributing photographers.

Either way, look out for useful clues about each photo library which can weigh for or against their inclusion on your shortlist.

Just as an example, take a look at the following extract from the Collections Photo Library (profiled in Chapter 1) website.

The site is essentially aimed at potential clients, giving excellent and humorous background information, but the library has thoughtfully included a page of useful information for potential contributing photographers:

Joining up with Collections as a contributing Photographer

If you would like us to consider your photographs for inclusion in the library please check through the following points.

We only accept pictures taken in the British Isles. We are not rabidly patriotic (far from it) but we just have to stop somewhere! We feel it important to have detailed knowledge of our subject to back up the pictures. Our files include landscapes, towns, buildings, people (of any race creed or colour), industries, events, traditions, almost anything that exists on these islands, though we avoid subjects, such as wild life or sport, that have specialist libraries of their own.

These strictures include the Family Life section which is much harder to get into, requiring full-time professionals who understand the problems which loom in this specialist field.

We do not have a minimum requirement for submissions, but we would expect you to have several hundred suitable images rather than just several. We do expect photographers to have at least one specialist subject or geographical area.

Please call the library and talk to us before taking any action. Do not send pictures to us without contacting the library first. We cannot take any responsibility for unsolicited submissions and you may be wasting your time and money (and ours) if your material is not appropriate.

(Extract from: www.btinternet.com/~collections, with kind permission of Brian Shuel)

Before leaving the Internet as a research tool, it is perhaps important to stress that the example of visiting BAPLA is merely a good illustration of what can be achieved.

Camellia x williamsii 'Anticipation'. Close-ups of fine examples of specified (and identified) floral species are in great demand both for specialist publications and markets such as greetings cards.

David Askham

Those readers whose life-style or business interests qualifies them to be known as globe-trotters, may like to explore photo libraries located outside the United Kingdom. The Internet may be the best, and almost certainly the cheapest, way of discovering libraries beyond the UK.

Shortening the list

The main objective is to identify those libraries which deal in your preferred subjects. With some subjects, such as travel, you may end up with a daunting list of potential contacts. In which case it is worthwhile considering such factors as a library's location, either relative to your home

91

base (for ease of access in certain circumstances, such as when meetings are important), or to their main marketing areas – though with modern communications the latter consideration is less important nowadays.

Do not rush this initial survey. You could conceivably miss the very one best suited to your needs.

The final step is to make a shortlist selection. I suggest that this number should be not less than six and probably not more than twelve. You may even consider tackling this in two phases; perhaps one phase of six, then if the first batch of enquiries contains too many disappointments, you have a backup group of libraries to approach.

Library information packs

As a result of the foregoing research you may have discovered that some libraries prefer an initial telephone call. If so, then take the hint, after you have prepared the ground.

The preparation for a telephone call is very similar to that required for drafting a letter. In both cases you will be requesting information and sample contracts for potential contributing photographers.

A letter should not describe your life history. Keep it brief and concentrate on giving relevant information about your kind of photography and specialisations. If your work has already been published, say so and where. It all helps to show that you have some experience. Do not send samples at this stage unless requested during the telephone conversation.

It is sound practice to enclose a large, stamped addressed envelope, though often this is not used, especially if the information you have requested is big and bulky. As a useful measure of a photo library's internal efficiency, note the response times.

When you receive the information, study it carefully. How comprehensive is it? How much of the information is relevant to your fields of interest? What is the minimum initial submission of photographs requested? What are the recurring commitment expectations? Do the terms of business seem reasonable to you?

Once you have this information, produce a table matching it against your criteria for each library on your list. This is a vital aid to the ultimate selection of a photo library.

A further word on your chosen criteria – if you consider one criterion, such as a wide acceptance of film formats or absence of exclusivity clauses, worthy of additional weighting, mark those columns accordingly. Then weight each criterion according your personal sense of priority values.

From prior knowledge of the libraries you have approached, and analysis of information received, whittle down your original list to about three photo libraries which most adequately meet your criteria.

It is quite possible that some of those on your original list may not require new photographers at the present time. They should be immediately eliminated.

Next, prioritise the short list using your original criteria, suitably weighted, to assist your judgement. Your first priority library will now be identified.

MAKING THE APPROACH

The next stage is critically important – the selection and preparation of your initial submission of photographs.

Although difficult to do – particularly as you recall all the difficulties and exhilaration of the actual photography – approach this task as if you were an independent judge assessing the true worth of the pictures, solely on their individual merit.

Picture selection

If possible, obtain a large light box with illumination of the approved colour temperature for viewing colour transparencies. Better still, use two light boxes; one for initial assessment and the other for progressive compilation of your submission.

Select twice as many pictures from your collection as the minimum number requested by your target library. You must force yourself to send only your best work and a well-balanced selection to show the range of your photographic skills, and each picture should be faultless.

Arrange the photographs in a logical order; for example, by subject or region. Next examine each one critically, using a good quality loupe, and reject any pictures which betray unsharpness, camera shake, unacceptable colour densities or casts, poor composition or any other defects. Only your best pictures will be good enough for consideration and to demonstrate your high standards.

If you use rectangular frame formats, remember to include a fair sprinkling of vertical shots. These have specific uses in graphic design, as in the widely used, classic A4 magazine front cover picture.

Gradually reduce the number of pictures to the minimum number requested. The rest, provided they are of good quality, can remain in your files for future submissions or your own use. Then regroup the survivors, by size, into logical sequences for presentation.

Presentation

If, for example, you are submitting 35mm colour transparencies, they look impressive if inserted into good quality clear plastic sleeves of the kind which present, typically, twenty pictures to a page. If you use this method, arrange the sequence of pictures to form a coherent and attractive set when viewed as a whole.

Ensure that the pictures selected are each individually captioned, or are clearly cross-referenced, to an accompanying caption sheet. Captions should be accurate, relevant, comprehensive yet succinct. If dates or seasons are important, include them.

Each picture should bear a label with your name and address – an easy task if you have a personal computer and labels such as those produced by Avery for laser printers or ink-jet printers.

Package the pictures in a strong envelope, with light-weight rigid supports to give full protection to the transparencies, and enclose your letter, documentation and return postage. According to your perception of the value, send by Royal Mail Special Delivery at the right compensatory level, or even hand deliver if this is an option.

The personal visit

If the response from the library is positive and encouraging, try and arrange a meeting with the library manager. The advantages are many.

It is an important opportunity to meet the staff and obtain a tour of the premises to see the library in action. It can be very valuable to see, at first hand, how well the library is managed, and to assess the personal chemistry of the people who run it.

A well-disciplined administration is impressive, whereas the sight of piles of returned and unfiled pictures would sow the seeds of doubt, no matter what the excuses given. If it is not self-evident, ask to see how pictures are processed into the library from their inception and through the various stages of marketing, accounting and storage. Discuss how new picture requirements are communicated to contributing photographers.

Prepare a check list of points you wish to discuss and be prepared for questions from them concerning your likely future commitment. As

Nelson's Column and Trafalgar Square from the air. The sort of **The Skyscan Photolibrary**
unique image that could only be sourced from a specialist library.

it is all too easy to forget vital pieces of information or observations, make notes during your meeting to refresh your memory and aid consideration of the facts after the meeting.

Unless you are remarkably lucky and find an immediate and obvious match, you could repeat this process with one or two of the remaining libraries on your priority list. In this way you will reassure yourself that your decision is based on a realistic comparison and objective assessment of the options. It is the penultimate stage before possibly entering a contractual agreement with a photo library.

Decision time

It is natural to feel elated at the prospects of joining a library as a contributing photographer and perhaps tempting to curtail the decision-making process. But before making a quick decision, refer to your original criteria table and amend it in the light of the new evidence obtained during telephone conversations, correspondence or meetings. Make sure that you have all of the facts you need.

Next, delete those libraries which do not meet your criteria and prioritise the remainder, according to points scored, taking account of those criteria which are weighted to reflect their greater importance to you. It is then likely that the photo library which most closely matches your requirements will be evident.

Advise the short-listed photo libraries of your decision and sign the appropriate contract with your chosen library.

Finally, do not dispose of the information which relates to those short-listed libraries which narrowly missed your selection. Retain that information for future reference as it could serve as a starting point if you need to re-think your strategy. Some libraries change ownership, fail, or terminate their business. If you are one of the unlucky contributors, your previous data packs and analysis will prove a useful starting point if you decide to re-open negotiations with a different library.

Profile

Corbis

Corbis is an interesting photo library because it combines the marketing of both "broad" rights (royalty-free) with conventional managed rights. Not many libraries operate in both fields.

Corbis was launched as a global library in 1996 and has grown by the rapid acquisition of existing analogue and digital image libraries. Thus, in a comparatively short space of time, it has acquired some 60 million conventional colour transparencies and black and white prints, of which a large proportion are already digitised and on line. It also has its specialist collections of royalty-free CDs, which in 1999 contained 12,000 images.

Corbis has approximately 500 international contributing photographers on its books and claims to cover all subjects, especially travel, celebrities, fine art, history, landscapes, science and natural history.

A study of sample catalogues and brochures suggests that many pictures are shot specifically with art directors' and designers' needs in mind. The accent is very much on generic images. There is also a strong American or international influence which partly accounts for global marketing by some thirty-four distributors.

Collections are produced under such topics as: Technology at Work; Currency Concepts; Just Flags; Family Vacation; Vintage Holidays; Everyday Mishaps, and History and Humour (some clearly betraying American authorship). A two-disc set of 100 images, with image files up to 32 MB, costs around $300 at the time of writing.

So I asked Anna Calvert, Sales Manager at Corbis UK Ltd, what were the main market sectors for Corbis images.

"We supply all kinds of markets. Probably our most fruitful are advertising, magazines, newspapers, books and television. The fact that we can offer both royalty-free images and managed license loans means that it gives our clients a choice. They are less likely to choose a royalty-free image for use in a prominent position in a document, because they usually prefer to negotiate time exclusive rights to avoid the use of an individual image by competitors. But for lower profile imagery, where generic images are ideal, they have a lower cost option."

Interestingly, Anna felt that fees had kept pace with inflation during the last three years, though perhaps too short a period for meaningful comparisons with other libraries.

Corbis computerised its library from the beginning, using in-house development teams. Intrigued, I asked Anna Calvert how was it that photo library staff had the time and capability to develop specialist software for library management?

She replied: "The owner of our business is an expert in computing. His name is Bill Gates!

"We have encountered no problems. We had a clear plan from the start and a belief that digital was the way forward. All appropriate functions are working to satisfaction and none remain to be developed. We deliver our images to clients on-line all the time. It is the basis of our operation; we are an on-line agency. We couldn't live without the Internet."

Anna Calvert has been on the executive committee of BAPLA for several years and believes that the organisation gives the picture industry a valuable voice.

I asked Vanessa Kramer, Managing Picture Editor, to explain more about Corbis' use of royalty-free images.

"Royalty-free pictures are managed by our American parent company, who select and produce about one new collection per month for worldwide marketing. If interested photographers approach me, I ask to review a minimum of around 100 images that could illustrate a specific theme. If the quality and content looked promising, I would send the pictures to America where a final decision would be made.

"Copyright of the original images remains with the photographer. Our customers are buying very broad licensed rights. So it is in our interest to select pictures, very carefully, which will appeal to a wide variety of markets. At the same time, we have to be extremely careful to avoid potential legal problems so images should be accompanied by model releases and other authorisations. We also need to avoid featuring branded goods and other elements which might limit sales. All-in-all, it is quite challenging."

So how are photographers remunerated?

Vanessa quoted the following example: "If a CD contains 100 images, of which 70 are 'Accepted Images'; and Corbis sells 500 of that CD in a quarter at an average price of $160.00; and the (photographer's)

Stipulated Percentage is 15%; the photographer would receive for that quarter $8,400, calculated as follows:

"500 CDs x $160.00 = $80,000

"$80,000/100 images on the CD = $800

"$800 x 70 Accepted Images on the CD = $56,000

"$56,000 x 15% = $8,400 photographer's royalty."

Finally, how did Anna Calvert see the market for royalty-free images developing over the next five years?

"I would expect to see more on-line single image sales. Already we have clients who wish to buy images selectively."

Clearly there would have to be a premium for such select use of royalty-free images, but that seems the way it is likely to go in the future.

5. Your Own Library

Although they probably do not recognise the fact, most photographers start their freelance lives running their own photo library. After all, when photographs are first sent out to clients in the hope or expectation that they will be published, invariably those pictures are drawn from the photographer's existing stock.

In those beginnings, when freelancing is very much a matter of trial and error, photographs are frequently stored in an ad hoc way, depending on the photographer's inclinations and circumstances. There is no compulsion to establish an orderly method of storing and administering the stock. But as the number of photographs grows, and business transactions increase, attention inevitably turns to inaugurating some form of disciplined administrative procedures.

This chapter deals with that transition and aims to cover most general aspects of running your own library. It will address how to set up your own photo library and run it as an efficient and profitable business.

That last aim is important, because unless a businesslike approach is adopted, the operation is unlikely to succeed financially. However, even if a library is not intended to be profit-making – such as when it is part of a charitable operation – it makes sense to organise it and run it efficiently.

The following sections have been structured to deal methodically with the essential steps necessary to an efficient and profitable operation:

Determining goals is an important first step. Unless you know where you are going, you are unlikely to achieve your full potential.

Essential decisions regarding both organisation and procedures are obviously important and unavoidable. The background to these elements has been covered in Chapter 4; here we relate them to the individual contemplating their own library operation.

Coping with the dual role. Attempting to combine the roles of photographer and librarian poses some important questions which are often overlooked during the euphoric stage of setting up a new photo library. Early failures can often be attributed to chronic overstretch of resources soon after launch.

DETERMINING GOALS

It may not sound like a particularly exciting starting point, but the act of deciding what it is you want from running your own library is a very important first step. The call for investment in capital equipment, stock, staff and personal time depends very much on what you hope to achieve and your personal commitment to attain that level of achievement.

If your aim is merely to gain limited financial subsidy for what is essentially a photographic hobby, then your commitment would be in a very different league to another photographer whose ambition is to develop and progress towards becoming an international photo library, perhaps one which could eventually be quoted on the stock exchange.

However, I would hazard a guess that most aspiring professional or semi-professional photographers stand somewhere in between these two extremes.

Why your own library?

Yes, it may sound defeatist, but it really makes sense to ask the question. Why do you want to run your own photo library?

If, after careful thought, you decide that there is insufficient motivation to face up to the considerable administrative demands of running your own library, there is no shame in deciding that you would be better off supplying an existing photo library.

It may be too early to reach a definitive answer to this question, particularly as there is more this book to be read. So it may be better to lodge this question towards the back of your mind for the time being, and address it again when you feel better able to assess the different options. Reading the profiles of real people may also help you to decide the most appropriate course of action.

An honest evaluation of your personal strengths and weaknesses should also enter the equation. Double-check the assumptions you may be making regarding any assets and help you may be taking for granted at the outset.

For example, will a spouse or partner still be available to help you in a few year's time? And if not, how would you cope with a sudden departure, through ill-health or other factors, of someone who is fundamental to the success of your business? It is tempting to side-line these considerations when the launch prospects seem so rosy and promising.

Your goals

So, let us be honest. You have had a few minutes to think about your goals. Have you decided what they are? If not, take time to jot down your initial thoughts.

But if after careful consideration you have to confess that you have no clear goals, it could be that launching your own photo library would be a risky business. After all, if you do not know where you are heading, you may be lucky but, on the other hand, you could be embarking on a quite disastrous journey.

Alternatively, if you have no obvious goals yet are still keen to run your own library, ask yourself: "What could be my realistic goals?"

There are many answers to this question, all coloured by our personalities, capabilities and circumstances. Let us look at some of the most likely motivations for wishing to run your own photo library.

Financial rewards

Probably the strongest motive for running your own photo library is the goal of maximising the financial returns on reproduction fees generated, either by marketing your own photography or the photographs entrusted to you by contributing photographers.

At launch you will probably only be marketing your own pictures, so there will be no commission to split with a third party. However, you have to bear in mind that you will be bearing all of the overhead and direct costs of marketing which will eat into your profits.

It would be a good idea if you carried out some trial budgeting to see whether your net profits would exceed the 50% share that you would receive from a commercial photo library representing you. This exercise would have to be carried out over a reasonable number of transactions and would only apply to those photographers who already have experi-

A specialist picture library may often grow out of a personal collection of local images.

ence of running their own library.

A second question to ask yourself is: "Would I achieve the same level of fees which a bigger library may be able to negotiate on my behalf?"

These are difficult questions to answer, but it is worth giving them some thought if only to satisfy yourself that you are aware of the financial factors.

Looking at the wider market

Most freelance photographers start marketing their material in a fairly limited way, a kind of "testing the water" approach. Not all succeed, becoming disillusioned by lack of success and fading away.

But many do succeed, to varying degrees, and are fired by the ambition to expand their marketing. It is usually about this time that they give serious thought to progressing beyond their fairly ad hoc methods and random operations and decide to formalise their operation by establishing a proper photo library.

For this group of photographers, a significant motive is to expand their markets to the point where a well-constituted photo library becomes a necessity.

Allied with the previous motive is the strong desire to increase the production of ever better quality photographs. This desire often springs from the increasing satisfaction from meeting their clients' needs and a generally growing demand for the photographer's products. The challenge of researching and finding new markets becomes irresistible.

There is no doubt that success breeds success and whets the appetite for continuing expansion.

Enhanced job satisfaction

Following on from the stimulus to expand the scale of direct marketing of your photography, is the enhanced job satisfaction which comes from running your own business successfully.

Many small business owners confess that they have never worked such long hours – or enjoyed what they are doing so much. This is not to make a case for extreme working hours; to the contrary. But the statement is often a way of expressing a deeply felt satisfaction with what they are doing.

The comparison really comes alive when a photographer has reached a crossroads in his or her life. Perhaps photography has been a spare-time pursuit used to relieve the tedium or uncertainties of less satisfying full-time employment. Redundancy, or the threat thereof, is often the stimulus needed to turn photography into a mainstream source of livelihood.

Which road should be taken at the hypothetical crossroads? The lure of greater job-satisfaction may be the principal motive for establishing your own photo library business.

Prestige

Finally, there is the prospect that running your own photo library will lead to greater recognition, possibly on an international scale, as your photographs are published and seen worldwide.

The values of pride and prestige are perhaps too abstract to be measured as motives in their own right. But they are nonetheless important factors which, taken together with other motives, add to the conviction that running your own library is a justifiable decision.

ESSENTIAL DECISIONS

It is time now to turn to more tangible topics and consider the actual wherewithal needed to support a professional photo library business.

Whereas a lone photographer can survive for long periods travelling around the world, virtually living out of a suitcase, a photo library requires a fixed location, office accommodation, and the necessary commercial equipment to support its business activities.

Establishing your base

The choice of location is an important decision.

The initial temptation is to adapt existing premises and, to begin with, this may be the only economic option. However, as the business grows, so too will be the demands for extra space, for expanding stock, additional staff and general office facilities. This should certainly be considered at the outset.

The other major aspect of where to locate a photo library concerns accessibility to your main markets.

In the early days of setting up a small business, it is natural to try to make the best use of available space, fitting in office and specialist furniture and storage facilities as best as you can. Thought is seldom given to the need for a reception area for visitors or toilet and light catering facilities, particularly when, at that time, there is no perceived demand.

As to planning for future growth and the possible employment of additional staff, well, that challenge would be met if and when the need arose. Even the possibility of transferring the business to new premises some time in the future is probably not given much consideration.

However, moving an established business is a major upheaval and carries the risk that trading will be disrupted, even if it can be accomplished over a public holiday or at night. The conclusion must be reached that it is far better to face up to potential future requirements for expansion sooner rather than later. Ideally one should choose appropriate accommodation, preferably with growth potential, early in the life of a new photo library.

Stock management systems

The heart of any photo library is a safe and secure filing system for stock pictures and a foolproof retrieval system. That sounds deceptively simple but it is far from easy deciding, at the outset, what kind of system to adopt.

Such systems should be capable of maintaining the stock inventory, raising delivery notes, recording picture movements into and out of the library, chasing up overdue returns, instigating the production of invoices, and keeping track of payments.

As part of this control process, pictures may be given unique bar codes to aid identification by electronic readers, thus avoiding tedious and error-prone keyboard entries of picture reference numbers and labels. That requirement may seem ambitious, but it is well within the capabilities of modern computer programs.

Not untypically with computerised systems, the experiences of photo libraries have varied. Some systems have been extremely successful, while others have generated their own fund of horror stories.

In theory, of course, there is no reason why computerised systems should not work well and become an invaluable and efficient aid to a photo library's administration. This subject has been addressed in more detail in Annex II.

Staffing

It is no exaggeration to say that most photo libraries are started by a photographer working alone. It is also a fair assumption that photography is their main skill and motivation.

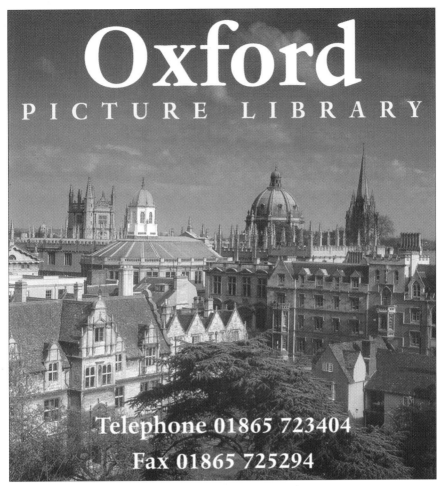

There is always room for the specialist library,
no matter how tightly focused the subject.

All the other necessary skills, such as administration, accounting, publicity, marketing and negotiation are acquired through experience and grafted on to the mainstream photographic work. Does this sound familiar?

So the question of staffing scarcely seems relevant at the outset. But the workload can become daunting. Much time may be spent away from the library, perhaps photographing new material, or visiting clients – while other customers are faced with only an answering machine. Picture researchers quickly move on to more responsive sources.

Two courses of action follow. Either the photographer realises that he can no longer cope with running the library and so explores the alternative of placing the work elsewhere; or he employs someone else to help maintain continuity in the business. Someone to deal, in real time, with clients' enquiries and day-to-day administration.

Any photographer seriously wishing to run their own photo library cannot escape giving early consideration to employing some staff.

So who to employ? Many involve a spouse or partner if one exists and is willing. A few are lucky enough to be able to bring a like-minded son or daughter into the business, provided they are competent and genuinely inclined towards the development of a family business. In any event, there has to be a high level of personal commitment.

But others may have to recruit total strangers, itself a challenging test of personnel selection and management. No doubt we would all rather be in a sunny clime photographing beach scenes and beauties, but unfortunately there are many mundane aspects to launching your own picture library business. You should not underestimate the amount of non-photographic work entailed.

Staff will require work space, possibly a rest-room, certainly toilets. They will almost surely need some training, if only on the nature and details of your business and the jobs you will require them to do.

Often your employed staff will be the human voice of your business, certainly while you are away on photographic assignments. They will need to project an image of efficiency, warmth, and competence.

Communications

Good communications are crucial to business success. It is in the nature of the media business that clients demand immediate response, despite the fact that material may then go on to linger in a seemingly interminable production chain.

So, in order to remain competitive, effective communications systems must be installed and operated correctly. Delivery of selected material must be swift, safe and sure.

The telephone system is still the most immediate means of distant communication. In parallel, the facsimile (fax) system is much used for transmitting lists of pictures being sought by picture researchers, and merits its own dedicated line to avoid communications congestion.

However, increasingly businesses are using the computer-linked Internet, both to communicate information (via e-mail) and transmit images to clients. Unit costs are considerably cheaper because telephone calls are charged at local call rates regardless of distances involved.

However, the transmission of photographs as computer graphics files takes longer than straightforward text.

Design for efficiency

Now let us consider the layout of your premises with a specific view of maximising efficient work flow.

It has to be said that it is easier to recognise poor layout than it is to design a good one. So where does one start?

The first step is to list the main work operations. This list will certainly include mail in, packaging and mail out; photographic stock storage systems; administrative desks for each member of staff; picture viewing facilities for internal staff; a store or stock room for backup supplies; a reception area for visitors with one or more viewing areas or cubicles for picture researchers (depending on the visitor rate anticipated) and rest-room or toilet facilities.

It is worth drawing a plan of the work space and even cutting out two-dimensional scale replicas to represent the major facilities to be arranged.

Visitor reception, ideally, should be near the main entrance and separate from the main library working area, even if this is achieved merely by screening. A member of staff needs to be appointed to act in a dual-role capacity, to be both receptionist and main entry point for incoming telephone calls.

Unless the work-load and trading volume justifies other arrangements, visitors can normally be scheduled, by appointment, to avoid both undue congestion and too much disruption of on-going library administration.

This area would also serve for meeting prospective contributing photographers, again by appointment, and viewing samples of their work.

Turning to the library layout, there should be scope for reasonable flexibility, although one essential is that staff whose work is directly involved with retrieving and re-filing pictures need to have their work spaces adjacent to the main picture storage furniture. This will avoid wasted movement between facilities.

Dealing with clients

No matter how talented a photographer you are, your success as a business-person depends heavily on your manner in dealing with people, particularly those who are clients or potential clients. The commercial stock photo library industry is extremely competitive and if you do not provide an excellent professional service in a friendly and personable way, there are many competitors who will.

It is hard to escape the fact that the personal chemistry between library staff and clients can tip the scales between success and possible failure.

A good starting point is the way the telephone is answered. To the outside world the person who answers incoming calls is representing the whole business, no matter that he or she may be the most junior member of staff. A pleasant and helpful manner is essential, as is a good grasp of how the business operates. If answers to incoming enquiries are not known, it is a turn-off for the caller to be left waiting, possibly listening to nerve-jangling music, for what seems like an eternity.

If a call back is promised, make it a firm rule that a return call *is* made. Library managers must be aware of potential business lost due to inept responses to telephone enquiries.

The main business of photo libraries is, naturally enough, to respond to requests for specific photographs. Clients will not thank you for sending vast selections of unsuitable material. So it is important to respond accurately to what is requested, and with quality rather than quantity. It is far better to send just a few pictures which meet the brief exactly, and in the process save time and costs.

Always deal with correspondence as soon as possible. Once again, clients judge a library on its efficiency in dealing with their requests.

Accounting

Only accountants will actually find this aspect of the business interesting. However, running your own photo library successfully entails operating it profitably. Without profit, there will be no funds for future expansion, or reinvestment, or retirement!

So it is clear that the business must keep a keen eye on its internal accounting.

Apart from the well-established accounting routines – including budgeting and frequent auditing of performance as a recurring routine – time should be devoted to scrutinising procedures and eliminating wasteful practices.

It is surprising how much capital can be tied up in superfluous or excessive stock, or telephone time on speculative surfing of the Internet. These are merely examples to implant the idea of reviewing procedures.

Massif des Ecrins, Savoie, France

Beaumes Les Messieurs, Jura, France

Luberon, Vaucluse, France

When a photographer becomes well-known, a library can be founded upon the certainty of quality provided by an established name and reputation.

Invoices should be sent out as soon as the information is available, with settlement terms boldly printed to help prompt settlement. Probably the most overlooked element of accounting is allowing overdue

111

accounts to run without scrutiny or direct action. Time spent routinely progressing debts is time well spent – in moderation. Sometimes it is better to place recovery action in the hands of professional debt collectors and concentrate on the business you know best. You may reach the conclusion that it is not worth keeping unreliable clients on the books.

Bad debts are an unavoidable bogy of business. There is usually no trouble in dealing with well-established business clients; problems usually arise with newer, smaller, probably underfunded businesses, whose ambitions outstrip their resources and capabilities.

How do you detect them? Only by asking some pertinent questions at the outset and limiting your exposure in the first instance. After a time, you will develop a "sixth sense" which warns you of latent risk.

If your instinct or knowledge identifies a risky new client, insist on stricter payment terms than usual until a satisfactory track record has been established. If this causes offence explain, diplomatically, why you are being cautious. Even if it results in a lost account, you may be saving yourself future losses and can turn your energies towards finding new and reliable clients.

Occasional analysis of your client accounts can yield useful information, particularly if you are able to compare the results over a few years. But I believe that it is important to schedule time in order to assess financial results on a regular basis.

Computerised accounting programs permit almost instantaneous reporting of cash flow, profit and loss statements, accounts payable by vendor, accounts receivable by customer, and the ability to assess any category of income or expenditure. Important reports can be memorised by the computer, and updated when retrieved, to simplify future analysis. Never before has it been so easy to obtain accounting information. All that remains is for the photo library to analyse and interpret the data and take appropriate remedial action.

Market research and publicity

Lucky is the photographer who can rely on requests landing regularly on the doormat. But it takes time to build up that kind of reputation and status. For the majority of small photo libraries it is essential to schedule some time, regularly, towards researching new markets and publicising what unique images and services you have to offer.

The problem is, where do you start? The marketplace is so vast.

One of the best ways is to select some of your representative stock, analyse it carefully, and make a list of all of the potential market sectors for which, in your opinion, your pictures are well suited.

For example, if you identify advertising as a target sector, break that down, if you can, into the types of advertising, by style or products and territories (global, national or regional). Clearly a photographer who has past experience of working for the advertising industry will have a head-start here.

Next study the market and identify advertising agencies, possibly in your local catchment area. Then select those which appear to match your type of pictures. You will then have a list of target clients to approach and impress.

How do you find the information in the first place? If you do not already have the requisite trade and professional reference books, visit a good local library. Once you have discovered some of the excellent trade reference books that exist, most of them updated on a regular basis, you may well find it worthwhile subscribing to selected directories so that your on-going market research is more easily done within the library.

But identifying potential new markets is only the first step. A great deal of work has to be done before sales start to be achieved.

So, is there an optimum approach?

Probably not. Although businesses in a specific market sector may appear to be very similar, they all possess distinct personalities reflecting those of their founders and their developing doctrines.

Creative people, who tend to be at the forefront of the commissioning or buying in of photography, are highly individualistic souls. It is almost impossible to begin to forecast their likes and dislikes until you have had the opportunity to meet them and discuss specific projects. If you accept this assumption, then it is clear that a route has to be found to the decision-makers in your target organisations.

Cold calling is not recommended. Time is wasted and a bad impression created. Far better is to design, or have designed, your own impressive marketing material.

Send samples out to carefully targeted prospects and then follow them up with polite telephonic enquiries to arrange a meeting. Little is achieved by just sending out mailshots and waiting for responses.

Where many businesses fall down in their ineffectual attempts at marketing is that they splash out on a campaign, possibly investing much time, money and effort, and then fail to repeat the process at carefully calculated intervals.

Of course, a first campaign may have been so successful that further marketing might swamp the photo library's resources. Generally speaking, however, libraries should budget for repeated marketing campaigns if only to replace clients who have been lost for one reason or another.

It is tempting to rely on published credits for keeping a photo library's name in print. Certainly that works quite well for editorial markets, but rarely works in advertising, public relations or corporate markets. But with the current high capabilities and affordability of modern desktop publishing systems, there is no excuse for small photo libraries not producing their own fresh, innovative, and highly professional in-house marketing and publicity material. This would make a significant contribution to their marketing.

Another possibility is the increasing use of the Internet by photo libraries. Already many library websites have been designed and are in use, with varying degrees of success.

In its simplest form, a website is little more than a colour brochure, waiting to be discovered. Any pictures included are indicative of certain ranges of stock held by the library. But some libraries are developing their sites quite radically, so that clients can not only view small picture samples, but download images directly for viewing or even use.

However, it remains to be seen how the problems of proof of usage, and accounting, will be overcome.

THE DUAL ROLE: PHOTOGRAPHER AND LIBRARIAN

Before any photographer decides to set up their own photo library business, they would be wise to consider, very carefully, some of the less glamorous duties involved, as well as a few of the unpredictable hurdles which can seriously impede or halt progress.

After all, it is a quantum leap from spending a high proportion of time photographing subjects out on location, to diluting that effort in order to organise and run a fixed-base business. There is a real risk that the photographic output will diminish unless specialist help is solicited to fill the gap. Balance may well be restored once the library is well established and competent staff recruited to handle the backroom activities.

The business plan

All new businesses require a business plan, regardless of whether or not external financing is to be sought. But why?

Without a plan, a business would have no predetermined goals and no structured approach to funding and realising company objectives. Only the founder will know, or think they know, what it is hoped to achieve in the business – and that will probably exist only as thoughts in the head. As soon as problems arise, or revenue falters, the founder may well flounder without a plan to guide the necessary problem solving.

A plan is essential for any business and does not take long to prepare, but it compels the founder to give some thought to certain very important questions, such as:

- What is the main objective of the business?
- How am I going to achieve that objective?
- How am I going to fund it?
- What resources do I have at the outset and what essential new resources do I need?
- What is my cash-flow going to be for the first year?
- How soon do I expect the business to be profitable?

Finance

No business can operate without sound financing. In the nature of the photo library business, income flows in many months after stock has been supplied to clients. In the meantime, staff and suppliers have to be paid and overheads borne. Financing has to be provided to cover this, not just in the start-up period but probably beyond.

If the start-up business operation is modest, perhaps using available accommodation and family help, first phase funding may be found from personal resources. But if the aim is to launch on a bigger scale, possibly in rented premises which need furnishing and staffing, then it is probable that external financial assistance would be required.

In that case it is imperative that a well drafted business plan is available to convince a lender of the potential viability of the business.

Coping with growth

A realistic business plan, sensibly and energetically implemented, should eventually lead to a flourishing business. Success, however, can lead to levels of growth perhaps not envisaged at launch. If that is the case an important decision has to be taken whether to contain the business at the fulfilled planned level, or to expand.

It is at that stage that the founder is faced with a dilemma, particularly if he or she is running the business almost single-handed. Can the founder cope with growth?

*Once a personal collection is well
established, it may be time to take on
other contributors. This became
the case recently for David Wootton,
founder of the Airsports Photo Library.*

The sensible solution is to take stock of the situation and draft a new business plan, because so many of the original assumptions may have changed. The discipline of writing a new plan will force examination of the many factors involved in managing further growth.

Writing a new plan is not necessarily a commitment; it can be an instrument of appraisal at the end of which a considered decision can be taken. However, if the decision is to expand the business, there is a better chance that it will succeed than if growth had been tackled in an ad-hoc manner without planning.

Business partners

Often sooner rather than later, many small businesses involve the commitment of a spouse or partner. Initially the contribution may be for no or low pay, at least until funds start to flow and profits arise.

It can be a testing time, particularly in the early days when there is little income. Long hours may have to be worked, not only in setting up a new organisation, perhaps in new premises, but in dealing with all the manifold activities involved in preparing stock photography for submission to clients.

There is also the inevitable learning curve as mistakes are made and best methods adopted. Holidays may have to be sacrificed and tempers may become frayed.

Of course, it may be plain sailing; just a successful coalition of existing talents. But the early stages of launching a business can be fraught with problems which is why a high proportion fail within the first year or two.

Insofar as one can anticipate the problems that might arise, it is worth thinking about how the personalities involved are going to work together and what are the chances of the relationship being harmonious and productive.

Health issues

The question of health may be last on the list of planning considerations before the launch of a new business. However the subject was brought home to me quite poignantly during my research into the changes which had occurred in photo libraries which I had profiled in my earlier book.

This revealed some sad statistics. Two key managers and one photographer had died, while another had suffered a series of strokes which had badly disrupted his business. Actuaries might not find this evidence surprising, but the experiences can be quite devastating for the businesses which suffer.

It is certainly costly, and possibly extravagant, for the smallest businesses to build in spare capacity to help overcome the possible partial or total loss of a key partner or manager. But the prudent might like to consider some kind of contingency plan to help the business to continue, in some form or other, if it is devastated in this way.

Managing staff

Not all employees are likely to be related to the founders. Indeed there is proven merit in recruiting new skills from outside the family circle. In some ways it is easier to manage staff in the latter category.

Good organisation becomes paramount when new staff are recruited to perform clearly defined tasks. It helps staff to know why the photo library is in business and how they can help to achieve the company's goals. Without good organisation and training the business will suffer from wasted time, resources and effort.

Regardless of background, staff need to be trained well in what they are expected to do. Training takes time and detracts from revenue-earning activities. But is vitally important that staff know precisely what is expected of them, while being given reasonable freedom to use their initiative.

A small team needs to become multi-skilled. Varying the work they are given to do ensures that when some members are sick or on holiday the work can continue effectively. Treat training as an essential investment.

Occasionally personnel problems will arise. What is important is that problems are addressed sooner rather than later so that they do not become even more serious. Indiscipline and absenteeism are particularly challenging and should be dealt with firmly but fairly.

Personnel management skills can be learned and applied with humanity. If successful in management, there is a good chance that photo libraries will avoid incessant staff turnover, which is a burden to be avoided. So select your staff with care.

Library associations

There are several groupings or associations of photo libraries, of which the British Association of Picture Libraries & Agencies (BAPLA) is the major one.

BAPLA is the premier organisation, with a good track record, and a dual-role photographer/librarian should seriously consider joining. So what can it offer the small or start-up photo library?

First and foremost, BAPLA possesses a wealth of specialist knowledge and can give invaluable advice to new photo libraries. It is a fast-changing technological world; businesses need to be kept informed and advised on how new standards are likely to affect their administration, and who are reliable providers of specialist solutions. BAPLA members' experiences are pooled for the benefit of all.

Many of the really important issues, such as the evolving laws of copyright, have involved BAPLA officials in high level and international negotiations on behalf of members. No photo library could afford the time to duplicate that work, even if qualified so to do.

In summary, a seriously ambitious new photo library would be the poorer without the backing and support of an organisation such as BAPLA.

Two other small associations of photo libraries were identified during my research.

The first, The Specialist Source, is a small group of around 30 specialist libraries which was described in the profile of Skyscan

Photolibrary in the previous chapter. Membership is by invitation.

The second is a rather different organisation of specialist photo libraries and photographers, called The Voice of the Specialist Libraries. This is coordinated by Lupe Cunha, an experienced photographer with her own library based in London. As part of the marketing and communications services provided by Voice, she also maintains a marketing website called SLDIRECT.

Lupe explains: "Our Association started with the quarterly publication of *Voice* and with the aim of promoting specialist libraries wherever they exist.

"At present (1999) we have around 150 members, but that number could grow as a result of our website. Numbers are unrestricted, but to take part in the Association's marketing operations members have to be running a specialist library, no matter how small.

"It is not exclusively for beginning libraries; we have well-established libraries as members. Another difference is that individual stock photographers can join."

For contact details of these associations refer to the Useful Addresses section of this book.

Profile

Charles Tait

If you think it is necessary to be located in a centre of publishing activity in order to run a successful photo library, take a look at Charles Tait's website (www.velvia.demon.co.uk) for a fresh view.

The web address does not give a clue that he and his library reside in Orkney, a remote outpost in the far north of the United Kingdom. So I asked Charles Tait whether his relatively isolated position had been a handicap in building up the commercial side of his library?

"Yes and no. The fact that my mainstream photography is localised to this remote area means that, by its very nature, it is rather specialised. That could be viewed by some people as being rather limiting. But the obverse is also true; that not many professional photographers can afford the time to exploit the natural beauty of this part of the world. Furthermore, tourism has developed greatly in the last twenty years."

So how has Charles managed to overcome the disadvantages of a remote location?

"Marketing is vital – doing a good job, giving prompt attention to requests, developing a distinctive style and, most of all, getting a name."

Perhaps the most important feature of his reply is the importance of building an impeccable reputation and becoming well known by clients, thus standing out amongst the competition. Such credentials are not earned quickly and need to be protected at all costs.

Charles Tait was a graduate in genetics and obtained a doctorate in biochemistry before working in France. A keen photographer from early youth, Charles became increasingly interested in serious freelance writing and photography before returning to his native Scotland in 1977. Then he launched his photo library and became a full-time professional photographer.

He has one assistant and is helped by his sons in their university holidays. The library contains around 60,000 colour transparencies in most

A striking image from Charles Tait's Scottish collection. **Charles Tait**

sizes, although his landscapes are mainly 6x7cm or panoramic format, with wildlife in 35mm.

The library's main markets are tourist brochures, travel literature, books, magazines, design and advertising agencies, as well as Charles Tait's own publications. The latter are a valuable by-product, and include tourism guide books, photographic postcards and calendars, featuring Orkney, Shetland, Caithness, the Western Isles and wildlife. How important was this publishing operation?

"Very – my own publishing business contributes by far the largest part of my turnover, although reproduction fees are also important."

In 1982 Charles began to computerise his photo library business. He bought a Commodore 64 and programmed SuperBase himself. All colour transparencies are now recorded in his database and are tracked through that program. Interestingly he is still using SuperBase, although he is in the process of changing over to a more modern program better suited to his needs. Only invoicing remains to be computerised, but he does use an accounting program.

Charles Tait took to the Internet in 1995 and found e-mail very useful as a method of communicating with clients. He and his sons designed an attractive website which, although only just starting to stimulate new sales, has proved cost-effective. A major upgrade is in progress, underlining the fact that websites need refreshing on a regular basis.

He has recently installed a program to facilitate file transmission and an ISDN connection which is already proving useful. The ability to do much work in-house on Photoshop and Quark XPress is proving very valuable.

The ability to deliver photographic images electronically is especially valuable to Charles Tait and he is pleased with his early experiences. He has encountered some problems with copyright violation but, on the whole, he believes people in the business are honest.

I asked Charles what advice he would give to a photographer who was thinking of setting up a specialist photo library? He pulled no punches.

"Study the market and choose your field with care.

"Do not waste time with substandard equipment – shoot the correct film and format for the market. Above all, shoot plenty and get out and about.

"Have infinite patience, steely nerves, and at the same time be nice to customers.

"Especially – be friends with your bank manager!"

Finally, would he recommend the field to others?

"Not really, as the market is so hard at present. Have I made any money yet? Not a lot, but I have lots of fun!"

6. The Contributing Photographer

Many photographers rule out combining their first love of photography with the demanding role of running their own photo libraries. They prefer to market their photographs through an established photo library.

This chapter is concerned with the psychology and attitude of being a contributing photographer and will try to draw from the experiences of established contributors to help the aspirant be more successful.

The chapter will emphasise the importance of understanding how a photo library works; maintaining consistency and frequency of new submissions; integrity; good business relationships; record-keeping; analysis of results; corrective action; studying market trends and planning ahead.

UNDERSTANDING YOUR LIBRARY

Let me declare at the outset that unless you have a good understanding of how the library to which you contribute operates – in particular its requirements and time-scales – you really are working in the dark.

Disappointment mounts through lack of sales. In consequence, as a result of lack of incentives, the supply of your new contributions will wane and your relationship with the library will become strained, possibly even sour.

I know this chain of events to be true from the numbers of photographers, over some years, who have expressed their disillusionment to me and asked if their experience is typical. This unsatisfactory outcome is much more likely to arise if new contributing photographers fail to follow most of the procedures advocated in Chapter 4 (choosing a library).

My answer to them is to say: Be pleasantly surprised with any fees you receive within the first year of your contract; in the meantime, keep submitting top-quality photography to meet the library's future requirements.

It really does take time for results to come, but by sustaining a good rate of new acceptances, so the volume of sales in subsequent quarters will reflect your industry. For the first year it is essentially one-way traffic, with you supplying new pictures and very few fees arriving. Unless you accept this situation – which frankly is little different to marketing your own material directly, apart from the added delay of the quarterly bunching of statements – you can easily become demoralised and give up.

Don't! Work hard at your project and review the situation after about three years.

Think long-term. If you have not been able to visit the library in person, try to discuss any doubts you have with the manager by telephone. But a personal visit may be well worth considering – I recall a correspondent from Iran who found it worthwhile coming to England specially to visit the photo library to which he was newly contributing.

Get to know the key personnel who select new pictures from your submissions and who can influence the way you work. Listen to library preferences; some advocate specific films to use because they know what their clients prefer. A change of film format may improve your chances of success.

But refrain from calling the library too frequently, otherwise you will distract the staff from selling stock pictures, which is their prime task.

Let us now look at some of these points in more detail.

Core stock

Find out which subjects your library currently covers and which are likely to expand. Try to gain real insight into the nature of the library's core stock and identify its main income-generating material. Discuss with the manager whether there is still time for you to add to that body of work, or is it essentially limited by saturation and over-competition. Clearly if the latter is the case, the chances of getting your contributions to that sector published are distinctly low.

There may be scope for producing a stylistically new slant which might go down well with clients, but do not venture forth on such a programme without agreeing, in advance, with your library manager. A refreshing new style is often of interest and is worth researching in an exploratory way. Libraries which develop innovative photographic styles can be very attractive to some picture researchers, provided the underlying content meets a publisher's basic requirements.

A more fruitful avenue to explore is to try and identify shortfalls in the photo library's stock and try to fill them. Most libraries have sections which may have diminished in value by virtue of aging film stock or obsolete content.

Travel is a classic case where the topographical subject matter can quickly go out of date. Many pictures' fee earning ability drops-off with time and they need to be replaced.

But it is a fairly logical conclusion that the more productive areas to be filled are those whose subjects are not so time-sensitive.

What is the competition? Find out how many contributing photographers are competing in the same areas as you intend to supply, so that you can filter and prioritise your own future work and contributions.

Some libraries try to avoid unnecessary duplication by limiting the numbers of photographers they will accept, but not all are so discriminating. If you sense that the competition is already fairly high in your main subjects, you may decide that it is better to turn your attention to other themes. Explore the possibilities with the library manager.

Quality checks

It is surprising how many photographers, mainly at the outset of their freelancing careers, have no real yardstick against which to measure their own photographic standards.

There are two aspects to this. First is the photographic quality, measured in terms of critical sharpness, colour fidelity and saturation. What may serve well as a projected colour slide in club or domestic situations may appear to be weak, or less impressive, when compared with other pictures on a picture researcher's viewing table.

The second aspect is the way subjects are taken. There are subtle differences between what appears to be a tightly composed, prize-winning photograph and one of near identical subject matter which has been more flexibly composed and is thus better suited for use as a stock library picture. What appears as wasted space in a composition may well be exactly what appeals to a graphic designer who needs that area for other graphic elements.

The best way of checking how your offerings match up to the competition you face is to ask a library manager to show you some sample pictures from their current stock. Look critically at the pictures and note the standard of photography, presentation and captioning. Ask yourself how you would have presented similar subjects.

Beware of the trap, however, of trying to copy style. You need to develop your own expressive style, but be mindful of the basic needs discussed above.

The time factor

Although the time factor has been mentioned several times before, there is very little that you can do to reduce it. Accept that long time intervals – several months at least and possibly longer – are likely to occur between a picture being submitted, selected for reproduction, and the photographer's share of the fee being received.

Why should it take so long? Let us start the clock at the time you decide to select some of your pictures to submit to your photo library. Unless you start editing your submission the moment they are received from your processing laboratory, there will be a delay which only you can control. Assume one week for the first stage, though it can easily become open-ended and stretch to months at a time.

There follows time taken in delivery to the library and a further delay until library editors work through your package and select the photographs which they wish to keep. Some libraries then return the whole package for you to cut, mount, label, list and return. Others perform those functions in-house. Either way, it takes time.

When the mounted pictures are ready for accession, they have to be computerised to join the library stock control system and then shown to internal picture researchers so that they are kept up to date with new material. Then they are filed. The actions described in this paragraph could take several weeks depending on the priorities given at the various stages.

Now the pictures are available for marketing. Let us take an optimistic view and assume that within one month one of your pictures is selected for a client's consideration. Unless it is destined for tomorrow's newspaper – unlikely unless you are supplying a topical news agency – there will be a further delay while decisions are taken. In book publishing this could be weeks or months because authorship and other production factors add to the long time-scales.

We will remain optimistic and say that a magazine editor likes your picture, along with several others from your library, and it is published within two months. There may be a delay of several weeks before the original images are returned to the library to be checked in and returned to the files ready for other clients to see.

Meanwhile the library will invoice the client and, with a little luck, will receive payment within two months. Then the library has to break down the fees earned from the package of selected pictures and apportion them to each of its contributing photographers.

How long has that taken? Probably not less than six months. It would almost certainly be much longer if used in books or advertising.

So the contributing photographer is not likely to see the actual sale on a quarterly statement until some nine months after submitting the original selection of pictures to the library. And that is a fairly optimistic scenario.

So, provided a contributing photographer accepts that there is likely to be an initial delay of up to one year before fees start to arrive, the positive aspect is that provided sufficient new stock is supplied the arrival of a quarterly statement on a regular basis should follow.

There is nothing like a regular cheque to stimulate greater effort!

Dead stock

It is important to recognise that a high percentage of pictures never sell, despite high quality or popular subject matter. The reason is that in many sectors there is just too much stock and therefore too much competition. Also, older pictures deteriorate, become out-of-date, or are replaced by better versions submitted more recently. Efficient libraries purge their stocks of photographs on a regular basis.

Many lists of wanted photographs are issued after a library has been unable to meet specific requirements. But it is difficult to judge whether these unfulfilled requests will recur. If they do, then the library is well placed to meet them. If not, those pictures which are produced specifically in response to "Wants" lists are filed only to stagnate without sales.

This brief explanation should help photographers understand why so many of their library pictures never sell.

Contractual terms

Study the terms of your contract and refer to it if changes are introduced, because sometimes conditions change as a library grows and develops.

For example, some photographers may be asked to bear additional costs if they agree to their work being featured in the library's promotional catalogues or CD-ROMs. This is a contentious issue, because many photographers feel that the 50% retained by the library from fees earned should cover the photo library's marketing budget.

Another point to watch is the limitation imposed by exclusivity clauses, whereby a contributing photographer is restricted as to further or parallel uses of specified photographs.

For many photographers this clause will not prove troublesome. But some, who invest heavily in global travel in order to update and add to their coverage, cannot recover their costs or make a profit unless they syndicate their pictures with the knowledge of the photo libraries concerned. (However, syndication is usually spread geographically, thereby limiting the risk of unwitting duplicated publication. In addition, care is taken to make sure that rival offerings are not identical images by, for example, changing angles of view or film formats – quite feasible with careful shooting.)

If you reach a point where you decide to withdraw your photographs from a photo library, be aware of the contractual notice required and the prolonged execution period as material is recovered from circulation as well as from an extensive filing system.

It is not uncommon for a year or more to elapse before all stock can be returned, particularly if some has gone overseas to related photo libraries, and most libraries specify in their contracts that this period be allowed for.

Copyright and Moral Rights

Copyright should not be an issue, as this is always retained by the contributing photographer. But contracts may now include a clause regarding the occasional loss of Moral Rights. What does this mean?

Photo libraries insist that, whenever possible, credits should be published alongside the respective pictures. But in some applications this is not always possible and the library has to accept the modified terms rather than lose a valuable market. In those cases, the photographer also loses his identification of authorship.

Most busy photographers prefer to receive good fees than worry about dented pride. But each photographer must decide their response to this clause, which is increasingly imposed by some end-users.

PROVIDING FRESH STOCK

On the face of it, this is quite a reasonable requirement and an important objective for the photographer to have in mind. Certainly libraries

Peak National Park, Hathersage, Derbyshire. Photographer Robin Weaver began his own collection by concentrating solely on the Peak District, but has since moved on.

Collections/Robin Weaver

would have a hard time if all of their photographers limited their contributions to just the initial package!

So it is not unreasonable for libraries to expect their contributing photographers to maintain a steady flow of new submissions, and accordingly most write their expectations in their draft contracts.

The flexible approach

After the first flush of enthusiasm some contributing photographers relax, particularly when financial returns seem a long time coming. The converse is also true: receiving a healthy sales return not only boosts morale, but stimulates greater effort to cash in on future submissions. Photographers with a professional approach invariably have an action plan which keeps them busy and guards against complacency.

Most serious photographers – be they professional or semi-pro – regard stock photography as just one element of their freelance photographic activities. That is a wise policy for several reasons. Until contributions to a library have reached the stage where regular and worthwhile returns are being made, and unless there are other sources of regular income to meet their total financial needs, photographers need to diversify.

Many in this situation undertake commercial or editorial photography which has the merit of yielding assured income in a far shorter timescale than pertains with photo libraries.

So, instead of viewing stock photography in isolation, consider how your other commissions, assignments or personal projects can yield suitable library material in due course, as a financial by-product. But watch carefully any areas where unplanned duplication of usage could lead to embarrassment.

Ethics and integrity

Following from the above, we should briefly consider the issues of ethics and integrity.

It pays to earn the respect of your clients and library manager by never giving a reason for the people you deal with to doubt your integrity. If you have the slightest doubt about the identification or ethicality of any of your pictures, do not submit them.

Maintain impeccable standards in both the material you submit and in supporting correspondence. Strive for captioning accuracy and timely responses to any special requests. But, in so far as positive identification of your pictures is concerned, do not give up until you have exhausted all reasonable research or avenues of enquiry. It is a value judgment how long you spend on this process.

Publishers and editors hate seeing identical pictures used by a rival publication. Make sure that you are not the unwitting supplier in such a situation. It can happen unless you exercise sensible controls over the photographs you release to the market. Photographers sometimes forget that they sent certain pictures to a publisher years ago, allowing them to remain on file for future use.

All of these considerations help to mark you out as an outstanding member of a hard-working and effective team.

Planning and anticipation

Plan ahead to acquire new material, preferably linked to known library requirements. Anticipate seasonal needs – recurring festivals, natural history, meteorological – all should be addressed to meet future market requirements.

If you are a travel photographer, plan your tours well in advance, so that essential new photography is assured and not dependent on unexpected free time in your diary.

Produce a written plan, major aspects of which can be entered in your desk diary as prompts for timely action. For example, in January every year I order new varieties of flower and vegetable seeds, pictures of which I know could well be requested a year later. Without such advanced planning those pictures would not be possible.

Remain keenly aware of current and local affairs. Read a well-informed national daily newspaper and a regional weekly. Watch local television programmes which can provide useful stimuli for events in your local region material suitable for submission to your photo library.

Taken as a whole, world, national, regional or local events should stimulate ideas for new photography, demonstrate new sociological trends or reveal unexpected developments. Never sit idle wondering what to photograph next.

Good communications is the key to building and maintaining profitable business relations. Keep your library manager informed of your photographic plans so that you can learn of any newly emerging requirements. Plan periodic meetings at the library to meet new staff and discuss future trends and likely requirements. Of course, this may not be practicable if you live and work miles away. Note, however, that even overseas contributing photographers take time to visit the United Kingdom libraries to which they contribute. No wonder they are successful!

Finally, obtain the library's wants lists and demonstrate positive reactions to new requirements by submitting new material linked to those current requirements.

RECORD-KEEPING

Keeping accurate records of business transacted is not the most gripping aspect of freelance photography, but it is an essential part of administration.

If you decide, after a few years, to withdraw pictures from an under-performing photo library, how can you possibly check the quantity and identity of stock being returned if you have not kept an accurate record of past submissions? What records should you keep apart from the financial figures needed for your annual return to the Inland Revenue?

I suggest that the minimum records should include: details of initial and subsequent submissions of pictures; details of pictures selected or retained; details of pictures published and the respective fees paid to the photographer.

Methods of keeping records

It may be helpful to discuss the various methods of maintaining essential records, especially for those who are just moving into full-time work as professional freelance photographers.

With extremely affordable personal computers available nowadays, there is no reason why all of the data and information you need should not be computerised. However, for those switching careers later in life and who still view computers with foreboding, feel free to use a manual system comprising correspondence, filing cabinets, index cards, statements, receipts etc. The choice is yours. Even with a computer you still need a modicum of office equipment to store records and correspondence.

Common to both methods is a simple filing system so that correspondence, submissions, receipts and sales statements can be kept together for easy reference.

It is a matter of individual preference just how detailed is the information you wish to keep regarding photographs submitted to your photo library. At the very least you need to know reference numbers, dates and short titles of each subject.

No matter whether you choose a manual or computerised system of record keeping, do make sure that the components of the system are likely to stand the test of time and that you have some form of backup in case of failure.

For example, a simple element like the composition of your picture numbering system deserves much thought to ensure that it does not become unnecessarily unwieldy as the years pass. Your recording system must be good enough to survive future growth of your photographic stock and markets. Before settling on a system, test it for ease of analysis.

Computers

A computer is first and foremost an efficient system for originating correspondence and picture labels, using word processing and labelling software packages. With suitable programs, it can also be invaluable for producing databases of pictures and comprehensive financial accounting. Most commercial libraries use specialist bespoke computer software for managing their operations.

Even a popular programme like Quicken can simplify a photographer's accounting and permit the production of a wide range of relevant reports in seconds, which can help with accounts analysis.

Two comments on conversion to computers should be made. First, allow plenty of time to familiarise yourself with the operational aspects of the various programmes you use. Do not underestimate the learning process.

Second, do not be tempted to upgrade your hardware or software unless you are convinced that the benefits outweigh the inevitable problems which arise when you change any part of your system. All too frequently immature software is released to meet marketing imperatives and end-users become frustrated with new problems.

This is not an argument against upgrading software or hardware; clearly there can be worthwhile advantages. It is just a cautionary note to highlight that it is not usually free from problems.

ANALYSIS

One of the secrets of success of some freelance photographers is the priority they give to monitoring their progress.

They do not spend a disproportionate amount of time scrutinising figures; far from it. But initially on a quarterly basis, and thereafter probably annually, they study their returns and their performance in different sectors, and make informed judgments which influence their future plans.

Analysis is essential in any business, large or small. Otherwise changes of direction or new priorities can easily be wrongly based on instinct, intuition or plain guesswork, with imperfect consequences.

Performance parameters

What performance parameters should you assess? I suggest seven parameters should be analysed, the first five of which are essential.

1. **Total income per annum per library** (or other independent client). This figure will reveal what each market is worth in gross terms; it does not take account of quantities of pictures held by each library. The spreadsheet could also show the income by quarters to aid calculation of the next parameter.

2. **Moving averages of periodic income.** Taken over, say, five or seven quarters so that short term perturbations are smoothed out and trends are more easily perceived.

Moving averages work by averaging an annual value over a number of years. For example, a 5-year moving average for the years 1995-99 would be shown against year 1997. This provides a better indication of trends.

Once income starts to arrive on a regular basis – and this certainly should be a major objective – you may find a pattern emerges when you look back over two or three years of quarterly statements.

Some subjects – winter sports photography for example – have a distinctly seasonal appeal and are less likely to sell throughout the year in the same way that a balanced collection of lifestyle pictures might sell.

If there are peaks and troughs in the sales reported by your library, and the variation is consistent year by year, you should consider whether you should be widening the subject range you submit to a specific library. It is still worthwhile calculating a moving average of quarterly income because you can see a clearer trend of performance which may be extrapolated to give conjectural insight into the future.

3. **Average fee received per picture sold**. A calculation of the average fees earned per picture sale in a library is a very useful figure to know.

Libraries may agree package deals with some publishers, which often diminishes the fees per single picture. In contrast, it only takes one or two pictures to be used as book covers or in advertising for the average fee to rise.

The figure is only meaningful if it is calculated over a period of several quarters. Certainly you should ignore the first few months after joining a photo library, when administrative delays prevent new stock being marketed and only a few sales are made.

But provided you are achieving reasonable sales every quarter, after two years you should be able to judge whether average fees are static, or rising more or less in step with inflation. By comparison with other data, such as direct sales or returns from other photo libraries, you can also judge how well the library is performing in the market.

4. **Average fee received per picture held**. Providing you keep an accurate record of the number of pictures held by each library, you can calculate annually what each picture on average has theoretically earned.

For example, if you have deposited 2,000 pictures and you receive £1,000 in annual fees for a specific year, each of those pictures can be considered to have earned 50 pence each. Of course this is a fictitious calculation and unreal in the sense that not every picture is sold. But the calculation has some merit because your investment covers the total number of pictures accepted by the library. (You bear the cost and responsibility for those pictures which are not accepted by the library but may be marketed elsewhere.)

One highly successful freelance photographer, who was featured in my last book, is very keen on this calculation. He uses it to calculate, after a reasonable period of time, whether a particular library is giving him a satisfactory return. He argues that if a photo library falls below a predetermined benchmark average earnings figure, based on competitive yields, and all other considerations being equal, he needs to terminate his contract and try elsewhere.

It must be stressed that action should not be taken hastily. The library needs to be given five or more years to perform and for the figures to be meaningful. Also, in calculating the number of pictures held, it is important to exclude pictures only deposited in the most recent six months, and probably also those pictures deposited for longer than, say, six years, when aging factors come into play. The population of pictures held is therefore a moving figure which is quite easy to calculate every six months.

5. **Picture submission acceptance rate**. This figure measures what percentage of your pictures submitted to a photo library are accepted.

This is quite important because, after the initial batch of pictures is accepted – which probably included some of the cream of your photography – the accession rate may fall away.

If a low acceptance rate persists, it could be concluded either that the you have not edited your work sufficiently ruthlessly before submission, or that the library is already well stocked with the kind of material you produce.

At least you can recognise the trend and take remedial action.

6. **Annual costs of supplying pictures**. We are now moving into more difficult territory where the photographer needs to be able to attribute production costs to his various batches of new photography.

All identifiable costs should be included, such as dedicated travel, materials, processing, equipment maintenance and repairs, registered postage and packing, etc. In order to know these costs, you need a system of apportioning them on a calendar or job-by-job basis.

If you are able to identify these costs, it should not be too difficult to calculate the average cost, per annum, of supplying a known quantity of pictures to the library. Setting these costs against annual returns from library fees will enable you to calculate the average cost per picture sale.

The choosing of an image for a library promotional card or brochure is critical, since it needs to evoke the essence of a collection in just one picture.

It is then a simple step to calculate the average profit (or loss) per picture per annum, and this figure can be used to influence the financial justification for continuing to supply pictures to a particular library.

Clearly if you you find that it is a continuing loss-making operation, you need to ask yourself whether it is worthwhile continuing.

Many "hobbyist" freelance photographers, who have other significant sources of income relative to their freelance earnings, may not be so concerned by the harsh economics. They are prepared to write-off their production costs and accept any income from photo libraries as a bonus. But photographers looking to earn significant sums from their library submissions really should examine the economics more thoroughly.

From the foregoing considerations, it is important to identify the key sets of information which you need in order to review various performance parameters. Careful planning at the outset is vital, because any later changes to your accounting system could involve time-consuming retrospective actions.

Select only the minimum amount of information which will enable you to measure your own performance and that of the libraries which are representing you. It is easy to get carried away with statistics and forget the purpose for which they have been generated.

How frequently should you produce the requisite data? Certainly on an annual basis. It will probably take three years or more before you can obtain a meaningful assessment of the performance of a specific library. But you need records from the beginning.

Example of a data table

Analysis of my results is one of my mid-winter activities when normal photographic activities are in a lower gear. For years I have used a computer spreadsheet programme (Lotus 1-2-3) to record certain figures such as:

● Year (or quarter);
● Number of pictures sold;
● Total fees received.

From this basic data it is easy, with a spread sheet, to calculate automatically the following:

● Average fee per picture sold per year.
● Moving average number of sales per year, measured over five years.
● Moving average total fees per year, measured over five years.

The hypothetical table might look like the following:

Year	Numbers of Pictures sold	Total fees (£) pa	Average fee (£) per picture pa	Average numbers of pictures sold pa (5-yr moving avg.)	Average fees (£) per year (5-yr moving avg.)
1998	30	750	25.00		
1999	55	1390	25.27		
2000	68	1724	25.35	68	1,756
2001	105	2658	25.31	77	1,996
2002	84	2256	26.86	86	2,257
2003	72	1951	27.10	72	1,912
2004	35	936	26.74	51	1,380
2005	40	1078	26.95		
2006	25	680	27.20		

Note that while the 5-year moving average figure is shown against the middle of five years, it is actually calculated at the end of the fifth year. So, for example, the annual fees received averaged over the years 2002 to 2006 is £1,380 and will not be apparent until after the end of the year 2006.

If you are familiar with producing graphs of data such at that shown in the table – and all spreadsheet programmes facilitate such presentation – you can see the performance trends more pictorially.

What conclusions can we draw from studying the above table? Well the most striking conclusion is that the numbers of pictures sold and the total fees received reached a peak in the year 2001 and then fell away despite the average fees per picture continuing to rise slowly year by year. In fact some action should have been taken in 2003, and certainly by 2004, to arrest the decline.

Market trends and forward planning

Part of the remedial action which can be taken to improve your performance with a photo library is to analyse the way markets are moving and formulate a rolling plan of action.

Markets are constantly changing, reflecting fresh fashions, novel developments, and new personnel with their subjective judgment as decision-makers. Suppliers to those markets need to recognise changes in the markets as soon as possible, otherwise continuing picture production may well be misdirected.

If you are preoccupied with other matters, possibly innovative technical developments in the field of professional photography, you may miss important indicators of significant changes in the markets you are serving, directly or indirectly through photo libraries. It is vitally important to recognise such changes, assess their relevance to your programme of work, and make the necessary adjustments.

You cannot escape the need to analyse the financial facts which relate to your performance with a photo library.

Unless there is something clearly wrong in the early days, allow two to three years, as a minimum, to see how the relationship is performing. After five years you should have a good idea of how successful you have been working with a specific library and be able to decide whether to continue with your contract.

Remember that disappointing performance may not be entirely due to the library. Ask yourself, have you kept up your side of the contract?

Some parameters need special scrutiny. For example, if your acceptance rate plummets, action is needed to get the operation back on track. However, it has to be recognised that the performance of libraries does vary with time as key personnel change or cease to be as effective as they were at the outset.

Photo libraries are no different to other businesses; management can be good, bad or indifferent. You must make sure that you remain working with an efficient and consistently high performing library and, for your part, sustain a constant inflow of excellent and saleable photographs.

Profiles

Instead of profiling just one individual at this point, I am combining in one profile two photographers who both contribute to the same library (Collections), but who do so from quite different backgrounds.

One is a full-time professional while the other is a college lecturer with a talented freelance photography background. Thus this double-value profile probably reflects a major cross-section of many readers of this book.

Profile

Robin Weaver

Robin Weaver is a full-time professional freelance photographer who integrates stock photography into his broad programme of commissioned work.

He studied general photography for three years at Newport College of Art in the early 1970s, to a present-day degree-equivalent standard. In his final year he gained a College Diploma in photo-journalism. This training led him into the press field.

For the next seventeen years Robin worked as a staff photographer on regional newspapers. His last appointment as an employee was with the *Derby Evening Telegraph*.

In 1992 he took the major step of becoming a full-time general freelance photographer, with landscapes being one of his specialist subjects. His income from photography now comes through sales of pictures from his own library to publishers of books, calendars, magazines etc, and from commissions from magazines and advertising agencies. He also undertakes press and public relations work for commercial organisations.

Robin uses Pentax 67, Bronica ETRSi (645) and Canon 35mm cameras.

I asked Robin about his professional work as a freelance.

"An early lesson I learned was not to put too many eggs in one basket. I worked for one particular client on whom I became too heavily reliant. Then one day he stopped using me in favour of a cheaper option. So now I spread myself as widely as possible."

Turning to his involvement with stock photo libraries, I asked Robin how he identified Collections Photo library as the one for him.

"I read an article in the BFP *Newsletter*, and knew it was the right library for me when I went down to London to see Brian Shuel and saw the highly professional set-up there.

The village of Longnor, Peak National Park, Staffordshire.   **Collections/Robin Weaver**
A fine and crisp seasonal image.

"Initially I offered the library my Peak District collection, but I have since added many photographs from all over Britain and continue to do so. I submit approximately 600 new pictures a year, of which 95% are accepted. So far the library holds 2,825 of my photographs."

The fact that Robin knows precisely how many pictures are held, coupled with a very high acceptance rate, demonstrates that his thoroughly professional approach to stock photography pays dividends.

"The results are much better than I expected. For example, my first cheque arrived only three months after joining Collections! This contrasts extremely favourably with a rather bad experience I suffered at the hands of another photo library (which shall remain nameless). That was a total failure. I removed my photographs after discovering a published photograph of mine for which I hadn't been paid.

"Communication with Collections is excellent. I receive regular newsletters which advise on what the library wants and, equally importantly, subjects to avoid photographing. If they have gaps in their files in my area of the country, they let me know and I always try and fill them."

I was interested to know how Robin merged his stock photography successfully into his broader programme of commissions.

"Unfortunately, I don't get enough time to devote to stock photography; commissions have to come first."

That is a frank admission by a professional who knows what his priorities are and what they should be. However, by skilful juggling of his time he is still able to turn in an above average performance as a contributing photographer to Collections and, in the process, has added a rewarding element of income from his freelance photography.

Finally, what advice would he give a professional photographer who is wondering whether to become a contributor to a photo library?

"Study the market. See what sells. Take lots of photos and several versions of everything. Be very critical of your work and throw away anything that isn't perfect."

How often have you read or heard these pearls of wisdom!

Profile

Robert Pilgrim

College lecturer Robert Pilgrim started freelancing in 1990. He uses 35mm and 645 film formats to photograph provincial towns to illustrate his lectures and for exhibitions. He also contributes photographs to hobby and specialist publications with a high degree of success, although he admits that sales only just covered his costs.

His main problem was not knowing what fees to charge, especially in the early years. He adds: "I was mainly self-taught, although I received help by talking to others and reading BFP publications. 99% was self-motivation." The latter statistic is revealing and should be pinned on the notice-board of every aspiring freelance photographer.

A significant turning point occurred in 1994 when, after consulting a BFP publication, he approached four photo libraries.

"All replied, but only two looked professionally run. In particular, Collections made it clear from the start what they wanted and the standard they expected.

"I had built up a collection of some 500 colour transparencies of follies and rogue architecture which I thought would interest them. Once I had visited them, I felt that I could trust them."

Within three months Robert received his first payment from the library. His 6,000 picture deposit now continues to earn him a return about ten months in every year.

Most important, he submits between 1,200 to 1,500 new pictures per annum and achieves an acceptance rate of about 85% – a notable achievement. He is clearly the kind of contributor any library would like to have.

Robert has widened the range of subjects he now contributes to Collections to include British heritage places and people, oddities,

Alice Through the Looking Glass, Guildford Castle, Surrey.   **Collections/Robert Pilgrim**
The sort of English curiosity that formed the core of Robert
Pilgrim's collection.

islands and "...anything I think will interest them.

"My bi-annual visit to the library is important. We need to meet primarily to keep in touch and avoiding my being merely a name. We also discuss future requirements and thus ensure that we both have a common aim."

So, how well had his experiences of contributing to Collections lived up to his expectations?

"Contributing to the library has made me far more ambitious in seeking out photo opportunities and thereby allowing me to sell more of my work directly – that is the subjects which do not go to the library. I am also getting an instinct for what is wanted, thus keeping down costs, and my work has improved. I am far more aware now that I am in business and must be cost-effective."

Finally, what advice would he give to a talented amateur photographer contemplating becoming a contributing photographer to a photo library?

"The photographer must know his or her subjects and aim to contribute at least 500 colour transparencies a year. Stick to one library, be dedicated, and do not be surprised to make a loss in the first few years. Remember, the library is helping you, not the other way round. And most importantly, your photographs must be of the highest standard you can produce."

The Nave, Guildford Cathedral. An image strengthened by choosing a time when natural lighting would have maximum effect in bringing out the architectural qualities of the subject.

Collections/Robert Pilgrim

FINAL CONCLUSIONS

Running your own photo library, or contributing to other libraries, is a serious business. Only those photographers who adopt a highly professional attitude – regardless of their day-to-day status – are likely to succeed.

For the novice freelance photographer, assiduous research is vital. Careful reading and study of the chapters in this book will help you decide which route to take, either the go-it-alone, or as a contributor. Hopefully it will help you launch a full or part-time career which can be highly rewarding, in more ways than merely financial.

Remember that the photo library industry is far from homogeneous. Like any business, you will find variations. People differ in their capabilities, performance, scruples and attitudes. So it is important to try to discover and work with those who are efficient, businesslike, honest, and who match your character and ambitions.

I hope that this book will have helped you to reach the right decisions and that your experiences in the world of stock photography will be as rewarding as you would wish. I welcome any feedback from you, based on your experiences, and wish you great success in your new ventures.

Annex I.   BAPLA

The acronym BAPLA (standing for British Association of Picture Libraries and Agencies) occurs many times throughout this book. Brief mention of BAPLA's aims and functions has been included in several chapters, but such is its importance in the picture library world that it merits more detailed consideration.

Here you will find a brief review of the organisation and what it does, as well as its views on the current state of the picture market.

Introducing BAPLA

BAPLA, the trade association for British picture libraries, celebrates its 25th anniversary in 2000.

According to chairman Lynne Bryant: "BAPLA is a communication network of professionals with a wealth of skills and knowledge of our industry. BAPLA is the focus that brings the various strands of our industry together and uses our collective might for the benefit of our industry and photographers."

Knowledge of BAPLA is vitally important for any serious photographer contemplating setting up a new photo library. Equally, potential contributing photographers to an established library will find it worthwhile visiting BAPLA's website and discovering which libraries provide information specifically for photographers.

At the time of writing BAPLA represents over 350 photo libraries in the United Kingdom. While this does not include every British photo library, most of the important libraries are members. Its authority and prestige are considerable, not only in the United Kingdom, but in Europe, North America, and also in the wider world of photo libraries and picture users.

Benefits of membership

Since it was founded in 1975 BAPLA has continued to expand its membership by 5%–6% a year. Interestingly, it attracts not only new libraries (or even ones still in the planning stage), but also long-standing libraries which have learned of the many benefits of membership.

I asked Linda Royles, Chief Administrator of BAPLA, why photo libraries found it so worthwhile to join the Association.

"Firstly, BAPLA operates a comprehensive telephone referral service for members, assisting picture researchers locate the best source of images. Many members report that over the period of one year, the cost of membership has been offset by the additional revenue and new business leads this service has provided."

The office currently receives over 500 calls per week. This has recently been extended to a 24-hour worldwide service through the relaunch of the BAPLA website (www.bapla.org.uk).

More specifically, each member also receives:

A copy of *Light Box*, a quarterly magazine showcase of news, images and features, as well as advertising for individual libraries. *Light Box* is distributed to design, advertising, and editorial contacts, as well as picture researchers.

Price Negotiation Guidelines – a comprehensive survey of lowest and highest prices charged for UK, European and worldwide image usage.

Free listing on the BAPLA website and web search facility, free entry and free copy of the BAPLA directory, and free entry into the European directory of the European trade association of picture libraries (CEPIC).

Weekly confidential update of industry news, events, and member to member communications on e-mail or fax. Includes legal cases worldwide, lobbying and technology updates.

Quarterly newsletter exclusive to members covering industry issues in greater depth.

Availability of NUJ/BPLC/BAPLA approved delivery notes and standard industry contracts.

Voting rights.

Libraries based overseas are eligible to join BAPLA under the Associate Membership category. Companies which are not picture libraries, but work in the industry, are also able to receive many benefits of membership and are eligible to join under the Supporters category.

Contact BAPLA for more details.

Advice to photographers

BAPLA operates a code of conduct which promotes good business practice towards contributing photographers, and each member is required to sign this code.

Linda Royles offered this advice to prospective contributing photographers:

"Do your homework; check that your photographic style and subject matter are in line with the photo libraries you plan to approach.

"Do speak to the library before sending any material.

"Do not send unsolicited colour transparencies.

"Do send tear sheets or colour photocopies showing examples of your work in your first communication with a library.

"Do read the draft contract thoroughly and discuss any questions with the photo library.

"If you would like more assistance, write to BAPLA and ask for the 'photographer's pack'."

Monitoring the marketplace

BAPLA is both a catalyst and a collector of information from its diverse membership. In 1999 BAPLA carried out the first comprehensive survey of the picture library industry in the UK.

I therefore put the question: What significant changes has BAPLA observed in the market sectors served by its members over, say, the past five years?

"There seems to be a demand for more and better pictures. As products and editorial stories compete for consumer attention, so the power and immediacy of the image has stand out every time.

"The technological driving force of our industry is probably the sports and newspaper sectors which demand ever faster delivery of images. But methods of electronic delivery, while commonplace in some sectors, are still frowned on by many who prefer a 10"x8" image to an electronic 'thumbnail'."

Other market changes observed by BAPLA include:

That the picture library industry is increasingly made up of collections focusing on specific markets.

An increase in contract publishing for corporate clients.

Growing awareness of the existence of photo libraries, but still some ignorance about how they operate.

An increase in the desire for "one-stop" shopping (for pictures).

A general increase in the use of modern technology within the industry as a whole.

So what about the future?

Future challenges

The biggest challenge BAPLA members face continues to be the extent to which they embrace new technology and the education of end-users; for example, how to down-load and use images transmitted electronically.

To a degree this problem is exacerbated by a lack of standardisation among databases, cataloguing systems, scanning standards and the different electronic methods of copyright protection (such as watermarking and encryption devices).

BAPLA concludes: "Protecting intellectual property rights, nationally and internationally, means not only getting to grips with the problems as an industry, but also with related legislation."

With such challenges ahead for the industry, selecting a photo library appears to be much easier in comparison!

Conclusions

In summary, if you are poised to launch your own photo library as a serious commercial venture, you would be well-advised to approach BAPLA during the planning stage. This independent, non-profit-making organisation, which represents the majority of important and successful photo libraries in the United Kingdom, can help new photo libraries avoid many of the pitfalls and give positive encouragement and advice.

However, if you are a prospective contributing photographer, do not expect that BAPLA can offer you detailed advice and information beyond their very useful photographer's pack. Recognise that the organisation's primary role is to represent photo libraries.

BAPLA cannot prove a personal advice service to photographers, but there are many other ways of finding the information you need, as discussed in other parts of this book. Rest assured, however, that your interests are constantly taken into account by BAPLA. In the long run, that works equally well for contributing photographers as for the libraries.

Annex II Computerisation

When I researched my first book on photo libraries and agencies in 1988, I found that only a small minority of libraries had seriously computerised their businesses. Looking back now, it seems almost unbelievable that electric typewriters and card index systems prevailed. Even the fax machine was by no means universally used.

By 1999 the situation had changed radically. Most photo libraries now use computers for accounting, correspondence, management, stock control, invoicing – in fact, most business activities that were done, or perhaps not done at all, by manual means in the past.

Computerisation is one of the fastest growing fields of technology. What is state-of-the-art today becomes obsolescent within months. However that fact should not deter businesses from investing in the best and most forward-looking systems they can afford. It is vital, however, to make sure that the software designed to perform the many functions in your library are capable of being modified and improved in line with future requirements. Careful choice of software developer and vendor is very important.

Computer options

Computer software programs designed for photo libraries provide a range of modules each dedicated to specific functions such as labelling, generation of bar codes and stock control.

As an example, let us look at the well-established suite of modules which Logic Information Systems Ltd of London has developed over the past ten years. The integrated suite is called PLMS or Picture Library Management System and its functions include:

Quick and efficient labelling, numbering and captioning of stock;

Automatic generation of bar codes for every image;

Comprehensive keyword search facility which can be customised to search selected data fields;

Comprehensive picture stock control system which generates delivery notes, reminder

letters, holding fee calculations and the recording of pictures returned to the library;

Meticulous rights control;

Detailed client and photographer databases;

Calculation of photographers' payments and release when invoices have been paid;

A full accounting package comprising sales, purchase and nominal ledgers;

Internal photo library management accounts.

PMLS is now in its fourth version and has been supplied to over sixty photo libraries in the United Kingdom and Europe. It is constantly evolving to meet new requirements and has been joined by two further programs:

AIMS (AXIOM Image Management System) is a complementary program which manages a digital picture library. In addition to the functions which are common to both programs, it also attaches a scanned image to each database record, usually as a thumbnail and a full screen image.

By clicking the right hand mouse button, an image is tagged and can be included in a group selection.

Search results can be printed either as a collection of thumbnails or as full page images.

Apart from conventional delivery, images can be transmitted via ISDN/modem direct to clients; or a CD of the chosen images can be produced using the AXIOM CD Browser.

The AXIOM CD Browser is either a stand-alone program, or it can be integrated with PLMS. It performs all of the many functions needed to produce a digital catalogue with keyword search capabilities for distribution to clients. Logic claims that the production of a CD using AXIOM is far cheaper than printing a conventional photo library catalogue.

Logic recently launched i-netcat, a new Internet software package which allows libraries to publish their image catalogues on the World Wide Web and allows potential customers, anywhere in the world, to access and view the images. New stock can be added to the database regularly, providing an immediate selling tool for current images.

Suppliers

Several companies have specialised in producing software tailor-made to enable computers to fulfil many, if not all of the functions listed above. For example, at the time of writing libraries have begun to use software to develop their Internet web sites to fulfil many more purposes than merely advertising their existence.

Because the software scene is so dynamic, BAPLA is unable to publish lists of approved suppliers. However, by its corporate nature, BAPLA does maintain a list of software companies which have supplied photo library members and can thereby help new members discuss their requirements with other members.

Comparing experiences can help avoid unnecessary pitfalls when a new library is planning to computerise its many library functions.

The future

If the past ten years is any guide to the future, it is difficult to predict what further beneficial services will be provided by computers and advanced telecommunications systems. Certainly the photo library industry cannot ignore what is happening in these fields, particularly now that affordable mature software programs are widely available.

There does appear to be an inexorable move towards full digitisation of photo libraries. Indeed, Richard Cruz, Managing Director of Logic Information Systems Ltd, fully expects that by the year 2004 at least 40% of picture stock will be originated, stored and transmitted digitally and that the percentage will continue to rise thereafter.

At present, relatively slow transmission speeds (between libraries and clients worldwide) are hampering progress. But when wide band-width transmission systems become available, at commercially affordable prices, it is possible to foresee many major photo libraries comprising large centralised computers acting as digital picture banks for direct access by clients. Now that is a sobering thought!

Of course traditionalists will always make a case for the retention of original colour transparencies and, for historical reasons, they will continue to be valuable library reference material whether subsequently digitised or not.

So, is the future entirely digital? Watch this space.

Glossary

Bar code

A pattern of vertical black and white bars of varying thicknesses, and numbers, coded to convey information about a product when read by a bar code reader. Used to store information identifying a specific colour transparency in a photo library and to aid internal management and accounting of stock photographs.

Caption

Essential information, answering such questions as: What?, Who?, Where?, When?, and Why? Included as a label and attached to a photograph, or detailed on a separate caption sheet.

CD-ROM

Compact Disk Read-Only Memory. A cheap and effective way of storing photographic images for distribution to clients for viewing and/or purchase.

Dupe

A duplicate copy of an original, usually a colour transparency. Strictly speaking a dupe will be the same size as the original; however it is not unusual to find 35mm originals recreated as enlarged images. Special low-contrast film is used in the process.

E-mail

Electronic mail normally prepared using a computer word processing programme and transmitted directly from the originating computer through a telephone network to another computer either within a company building or anywhere worldwide.

Fax

Abbreviation for facsimile transmission. A means whereby information including graphics is transmitted and received, electronically, over distances, yielding a reasonable 'facsimile' likeness to the original. Stand alone fax machines were once needed, but now the same task can be accomplished directly between computers, or computers and facsimile terminals.

Holding fee

A fee charged by a photo library for photographs held by a client beyond a specified or agreed period of time.

ISDN

Integrated Services Digital Network. Telecoms technology permitting faster rates of data transmission.

Light box

A back-illuminated opaque flat glass or plastic surface used for viewing colour transparencies. It can be contained in a portable or fixed box, or built into a viewing table. The illuminating source is colour balanced to match correctly exposed film stock.

Loupe (or **lupe**)

High quality optical magnifier used for examinining colour transparencies on a light box.

Media

Means by which an image, thought or sound is communicated. In the context of this book, the media is generally accepted as books, magazines, newspapers, advertising or television.

Model release

Written agreement, signed by a named and identified model, authorising photographs of that model to be used in specified media or for a specific purpose.

Moral Rights

The Copyright Act of 1988 confers three moral rights: The right of paternity, requiring a photographer to be identified along with the reproduction of their work; the right of integrity, safeguarding against distortion or unauthorised alteration of the photographer's work; the right not to have work falsely attributed to you.

Photo library
See Stock Picture Library.

Photo agency
An agency representing one or more photographers, either in the role of obtaining photographic assignments, or reproduction rights for the photographer's work, or both.

Rights
Specified and agreed conditions for the use of photographs in identified media. Rights will be qualified in a more detailed way, For example, by specifying territorial, time and media factors. Single Reproduction Rights; United Kingdom Rights; World Rights; Full Copyright, are examples. It is extremely rare for Full Copyright to be sold by a library.

Service fee
A fee charged by a photo library to cover the time and administration costs for picture research prior to supplying photographs to a client.

Slide
Transparency, usually colour, used in publishing or projection.

Software
Generic term used for computer programmes and associated documentation.

Stock picture library
A library of photographic images, usually in the form of colour transparencies or monochrome prints, the product of the owner or contributing photographers or both. The photographs are available for loan on payment, for use in the various forms of media or publication.

Subject index
A list of photographic subjects held by a photo library, arranged generically, alphabetically or in other specified order to facilitate easy reference and picture retrieval.

Tranny
A slang term for transparency, usually a colour transparency.

Useful Addresses

British Association of Picture Libraries and Agencies (BAPLA)
18 Vine Hill, London EC1R 5DZ.
Tel: 020 7713 1780. Fax: 020 7713 1211. E-mail: bapla@bapla.org.uk
www.bapla.org.uk

Bureau of Freelance Photographers (BFP)
Focus House, 497 Green Lanes, London N13 4BP.
Tel: 020 8882 3315. Fax: 020 8886 5174.
www.thebfp.com

Coordination of European Picture Agencies (CEPIC)
Teutonenstr. 22, 14129 Berlin, Germany.
Tel: +49 30 816 99429. Fax: +49 30 816 99445. E-mail: cepic@akg.de
www.cepic.org

Design & Artists Copyright Society (DACS)
Parchment House, 13 Northburgh Street, London EC1V 0AH.
Tel: 020 7336 8811. Fax: 020 7336 8822.

National Association of Press Agencies (NAPA)
41 Lansdowne Crescent, Leamington Spa, Warwickshire CV32 4PR.
Tel: 01926 424181. Fax: 01926 424760.

National Union of Journalists (NUJ)
Acorn House, 314 Gray's Inn Road, London WC1X 8DP.
Tel: 020 7278 7916. Fax: 020 7278 1812.

Picture Agency Council of America (PACA)
P.O.Box 308, Northfield, MN 55057-0308, USA.
Tel: 800 457 7222. Fax: 800 645 7066.
www.indexstock.com/pages/paca.htm

Picture Research Association (PRA)
The Studio, 5a Alvanley Gardens, London NW6 1JD.
Tel: 020 7431 9886. Fax: 020 7431 9887.
E-mail: pra@pictures.demon.co.uk

Presse Informations Agentur GmbH (PIAG)
Stefanienstr. 25, D-76530 Baden-Baden, Germany.
Tel: +49 7221 301 7560. Fax: +49 7221 301 7561.
E-mail: piag.visuell@t-online.de
www.piag.de

Professional Photographic Laboratories Association (PPLA)
29 Hempfield Road, Littleport, Ely, Cambs CB6 1ND.
Tel: 01353 863255. Fax: 01353 863522.

Voice of the Specialist Libraries
Photo-Arte Gallery, 19 Ashfield Parade, London N14 5EH.
Tel: 020 8882 6441. Fax: 020 8882 6303.
E-mail: lupe.cunha@btinternet.com
www.sldirect.co.uk

Index